Following a career in foreign exchange both in the City of London and the Middle East, J.A. Payne started and ran a successful business. He retired in 2006 and lives with his wife Jude in Essex.

A RELUCTANT GUEST

A RELUCTANT GUEST

Taken Hostage by Saddam Hussein

J.A. PAYNE

GREENWICH EXCHANGE
LONDON

Greenwich Exchange, London

First published in Great Britain in 2020
New edition published 2022
All rights reserved

Printed and bound by imprintdigital.com

Greenwich Exchange Website: www.greenex.co.uk

Cataloguing in Publication Data
is available from the British Library

Cover materials: Shutterstock

ISBN: 978-1-910996-65-2

CONTENTS

Foreword

Since my return from banking in the Middle East, I have regaled friends and acquaintances with different stories of my time there. 'Write a book,' they said. 'Get these stories down!' After decades of procrastination I eventually completed this recollection.

This book was completed during the first Covid lockdown. Being locked away along with the rest of the UK was the perfect time to write and allowed some respite from obsessing about the awful pandemic.

The narrative attempts to convey the prevailing atmosphere of the time and place. Employed as a foreign exchange dealer in Kuwait, I enjoyed a privileged lifestyle until the Iraq army invaded on 2 August 1990. My following experiences of hiding, capture and being taken hostage on the 'Human Shield' is in stark contrast.

From the tanks rumbling down the Gulf Street to the end of the tale, I refer to copious notes recorded at the time and believe the account and chronology to be correct. When penning my life in Kuwait before the invasion I decided to enliven the tale by using experiences and anecdotes collected over a decade in banking around the Gulf. Indeed I place myself employed by the fictitious MBME (an acronym for Many Banks of the Middle East). Mr John Henry, Mr Zamir Shadid and Susan are pseudonyms. Other characters are written using their first name. In the words of the great Eric Morecambe, 'I'm telling all the right stories but not necessarily in the right order.'

Thanks to my wife Jude and daughters Charlotte and Emily who encouraged me throughout. I also owe a debt of gratitude to Peter Randall who first suggested the book over twenty years ago. Peter and everyone at Greenwich Exchange were unwavering in their support. Finally I would like to acknowledge the many appearing in this book not listed below.

Fellow hostages: Colin, Patrick, Malcolm, Willie and Alfred.

Friends in hiding: Martin, Ray, Virgie, Gloria, Waleed, Steve, Bushby, Ali and Lorraine.

1
The Job Interview

The concrete covered ground, together with brick and glass buildings, radiated intense heat. The air shimmered in the small compound and like a caged animal, I circled the yard drenched in sweat, attracting flies. Thoughts rushed around my head disappearing as quickly as they came. Shit, shit, shit and double shit! How on earth did it come to this? Why was I here in Iraq? Why me? I had to somehow come to terms with what was happening. The why I was here was easy enough ...

The day was particularly manic with the US dollar going up and down like a 'whore's drawers', as the traders used to say. Phones were alive, mostly clamped to dealers' ears as various numbers were screamed towards the spot desk. These prices were dealt with a wave of the hand or left alone with a shake of the head. The atmosphere was electric in the dealing room with computer screens flashing changes, desperately trying to keep up with the moving markets. The excitement was alluring but rather than get involved, I was keeping my head down and protecting my profits. Leaving the bank around six pm, I made my way to the Underground.

As the train rattled along the Central line I was annoyed with myself for once again not leaving more time to make my meeting, a failing I was often guilty of. Perhaps it was something in my DNA, a hereditary thing. My uncle suffered with the same problem and once got caught on a train after seeing my brother and myself onto the overnight sleeper from Dundee to King's Cross. The next stop was Leuchars six miles away and Steve and I being twelve and ten at the time found it hilarious. My uncle, of course, blamed the large Pakistani family who filled the whole corridor after boarding at the last minute. My uncle was shouting all sorts of abuse at them – it was 1969 and no one batted an eyelid. We were wetting ourselves with laughter.

My appointment at Claridge's in Mayfair was for 6.45pm and it was now half past. It was going to be a close thing. I had to hotfoot it to the hotel in Brook Street and then compose myself before the job interview with Mr Zamir Shadid. Two weeks prior to this meeting I approached a recruitment agent who specialised in both banking and international placements. Being a child born to expatriate parents, I was keen to work somewhere warmer and where the commuting ... well, the less said about that the better!

I liked being one of 'Maggie's Boys', a mid-twenties foreign exchange dealer in the city with an appetite for life. What I did not appreciate was the government taking as much of my income and, when it came to bonuses, more of my hard-earned cash than myself. I believed a tax-free position abroad for a few years might help me accumulate some personal wealth and take me away from the drug- and alcohol-fuelled lifestyle I was currently living.

Having told the head-hunter that I was interested in the Far East or possibly Australia, perversely, he called to suggest a position at The MBME Bank, Kuwait.

'Have you heard of Kuwait? Do you know where it is?'

I told him that I was born in Kuwait and recalled wonderful childhood memories of the place.

'Marvellous coincidence, old boy,' he said.

He asked me to meet Mr Shadid – sometimes referred to as Crazy Harry.

'I'm sure you two will get on famously.'

Mr Shadid acquired a well-earned reputation as an international trader because of the large unhedged positions he took in the currency markets. Occasionally his appetite for risk, coupled with his style of proprietary dealing, showed just how he had earned his nickname.

It was a typical British summer and we were experiencing a relentless drizzle. I arrived at Claridge's a bit dishevelled with three minutes to spare. I approached reception and asked them to inform Mr Shadid that Mr Payne was waiting for him. A short time later the two of us were seated in the lobby enjoying some excellent coffee. After various pleasantries where the fact that I was born in Kuwait was raised, we got down to the nitty gritty of the interview. We hit it off and an hour later he produced a standard contract which I signed after a few alterations. He must have been keen because a week later two copies of the contract, signed by the General Manager, landed on my doorstep, one to keep and one to sign and return.

I left Claridge's walking on a small cushion of air and entered the first bar I came across. I ordered a pint, paid the barman and went straight to the toilet where I consumed a large line of cocaine. I felt euphoric and any doubts about the change in my life's direction would come later but for the moment, I wanted to get back to my local pub and quaff a few with the other barflies. I planned to follow this up with a visit to a curry house followed by a bit of late night telly.

Next morning, I woke with a fierce hangover to the sound of the buzzer informing me someone was at the front door of my block of flats.

'Yeah, who is it?'

'It's only meee!'

I pressed the entry button and opened the door. I donned a bathrobe covering my modesty and went into the kitchen to put on a pot of coffee.

Bob the DJ entered my flat, took one look at me and grinned.

'You look like shit.'

Even though my head was throbbing and I felt decidedly shabby, I managed to smile back.

'Thank you very little! I think I overdid it a bit last night, far too much of everything. Do you want a coffee?'

'Cheers,' he replied as he sat down and started to build a joint.

Bob had become a good mate over the last year or so and lived close by. He made a modest income as a DJ in some of the less salubrious pubs and clubs in the area but not enough to keep him. His earnings were supplemented by a variety of nefarious activities. He was known as a bit of a hard man with a colourful history. Following a violent altercation, he served a stretch at Her Majesty's Pleasure. A bad scar was mostly hidden by his hair. He had been hit by a metal bar before he ended the fight with a stabbing, which left his opponent in intensive care.

He was well known in the area and, as we were often together, the local street life showed me a modicum of respect. We lived in a fairly tough part of South London but I always felt safe enough.

As I poured the coffee Bob asked me about the interview.

'Not too bad. Not only was I offered the job but we thrashed out a contract as well.'

'Nice one, mate. When are you off?' he asked trying to pass me the spliff.

'Hopefully about three or four weeks,' I replied whilst refusing the dope on offer.

'Christ! You must be bad,' he said, almost pissing himself with laughter.

'I need a couple more hours of shut-eye followed by a bath and then I'll be ready for a celebration if you're up for it?'

He suggested a return to my flat early evening. With that he left and I went back to bed.

I awoke much later and microwaved the remains of the previous night's Indian take-away. Having completed the standard ablutions, I made a few phone calls. The first was to my girlfriend Mandy to tell her my good news; not so good for her apparently, as we argued and she slammed the phone down on me. Following three more phone calls to my father, brother and best mate Mac, I called Bob and suggested we go on the piss.

Bob was back.

'How are you going to manage without the drugs when you get to the desert?'

I told him that one of the main reasons for leaving the city and going to the Middle East to work was to dry out a bit and hopefully put pills and powders behind me forever. I explained this was not a lifestyle choice but more like a lifesaving decision!

He chuckled and started to roll a spliff as I sat down with a credit card to chop two lines of cocaine.

'What are you going to do with your flat while you're away?'

I discussed the pros and cons of renting it out and he said that he was interested. I was not sure this was a good idea and muttered that I would mull it over. Bob put two or three ready-rolled joints into an empty packet of Benson & Hedges and we left the flat. We got into Bob's car and made our way to The Simla which was our pub of choice at that time.

During the following weeks I made various preparations including a medical and filling in endless paperwork. The bundle of forms included a copy of my birth certificate and the relevant pages of my passport. I was just waiting for the results of my medical. Once that arrived, I could send it all to the bank in Kuwait where they would do the necessary in acquiring a work permit and residency for me.

I felt I could tick off two items on my 'to-do list' and headed off to Oxford Street. A couple of lightweight suits and a suit carrier were essential and included on my shopping list. The horrible chore completed, I made my way to the City to meet Mandy in Dirty Dick's, a pub close to Liverpool Street station. The plan was to have a few drinks followed by a meal and then back to the flat. It may sound callous that meeting my girlfriend was on my 'to-do list', but truth being told, I was nervous about our date. My trepidation was due to several heated phone conversations following my news.

The evening was a bit tense and we both started to drink like rugby players on tour. However hard I tried to move the conversation to topics other than my move to the Middle East, the elephant in the room couldn't be avoided. The inevitable confrontation occurred in the curry house at the end of my road. We consumed more alcohol and were waiting for the food to arrive. She could no longer contain herself and played to a ready-made audience in the nearly full restaurant.

'So how long is this contract for, then?' she slurred in a loud, belligerent voice.

'Can't we leave this until we get back to the flat?' I begged.

'No we fucking can't!' she shouted.

The restaurant went quiet and I went a shade of red normally reserved for sunburn.

'Please don't do this now. We'll be back in the flat in a bit,' I simpered.

'No! Come on, tell me! How long is this contract for?' she enunciated each word loudly.

'Any chance you could do our food to go?' I asked one of the waiters.

He nodded and scuttled off to the kitchen.

'Three years,' I almost whispered.

My answer to her question was met with an attempt at sarcasm, albeit very slurred. The waiter rushed to our table with the food and the bill which I paid with equal alacrity in cash so that I could grab Mandy and the parcel of food and usher them both out of the door.

Back at the flat Mandy seemed to have calmed down a bit and was attempting to talk reasonably. We established that she was not coming to the Middle East with me and she also let me know in no uncertain terms, that if I thought she would be waiting around for three years, I had another think coming!

We attempted to watch a film in a stony silence. I certainly couldn't concentrate and she nodded off. I rolled and smoked a couple of joints before waking her. We went to bed and put our differences aside, making up in the way lovers have throughout history. The next morning, following lots of tears and empty promises, we agreed to try to make it work. She left the flat and I felt empty, depressed and a little relieved all at the same time.

Later that same morning I received a phone call from the private clinic that conducted my medical testing for every disease known to man – and of course HIV/AIDS. This was a very scary proposition in the eighties. They requested I come to the clinic for my results. I asked them if they could just post them to me.

'No. You have to come in and see us,' the person on the phone responded.

I asked if the tests were negative.

'You will have to come in and see us.'

My heart missed a beat. Feeling sick and having convinced myself I was HIV positive, I asked to attend the clinic immediately. Getting into my car and doing an impression of James Hunt, I got to the clinic within twenty minutes. I was almost a basket case by now and waiting in reception seemed interminable. They eventually ushered me into a room and the doctor gave my results and told me everything was fine.

'What do you mean fine?' I yelled with steam coming out of my ears. 'If everything is fine and I don't have AIDS, why didn't you just tell me over the phone?' I may have added a few expletives.

The doctor definitely did not appreciate my rudeness but, with some sympathy, explained it was a government directive as anyone who did have HIV/AIDS should be told in person in case they became suicidal with the news. I left the clinic truly elated.

2
A Weekend in Bournemouth

Noon on Friday I headed off to Waterloo to catch the train to Bournemouth. I wanted to miss the weekend rush and meet up with my best friend. We met at school when we were twelve and had been good pals ever since. I knew we were in for the usual shenanigans which always seemed to occur when we got together.

Enjoying a drink since our teens, we had drifted into socially using cannabis and occasionally cocaine. Mac was disciplined and managed his life balance very well. He worked hard, enjoyed a loving family and reserved his benders for 'high days and holidays'. I played rugby at college and enjoyed a beer-soaked social life. Once employed in the City, I was easily led into a hard-drinking culture, and beer was replaced with vodka as my drink of choice. Cocaine was rife in the City in the eighties and, unlike my pal, I was using more and more frequently. The decision to leave the UK was a good one but until the flight I planned to thoroughly enjoy myself. Hopefully we were in for a high day!

The train journey passed pleasantly enough with no delays

and I arrived in Bournemouth mid-afternoon. Mac was waiting for me at the station.

'You alright then, mush?' He loved a bit of Dorset slang.

'What's the big news then?'

I chucked my overnight bag in the back of his van and jumped into the passenger seat. Lighting a joint and passing it straight to Mac I answered, 'Yeah, all good, mate. I'll give you the lowdown when we hit the boozer.'

The boozer was The Cricketers which we had been frequenting since we were about sixteen and where we felt like part of the furniture. I just loved being in there early Friday evening when the locals started arriving straight from work, all in a good mood anticipating the weekend. The banter was usually excellent with various humorous themes from years gone by resurrected along with any new issues of comic interest. As we drove straight past the road leading towards the pub, I said with a cheeky grin, 'You must be distracted, mate. You've missed the turning.'

'Twat,' was his reply after a chortle.

'We'll drop your bag and you can have a catch up with Carole. She can drop us at the pub about five. Does that meet with your approval, Mr Payne?'

'Yeah, course. How is Carole?'

'All good, mate. All good.'

The three of us sat in the kitchen and Carole made a pot of tea. Mac and I started our usual comic banter. Carole, bless her, had heard it all before and under a pretext of 'things to do', disappeared out of the kitchen.

'Well, shall we head off to the Cricks?' asked Mac.

I pulled out a wrap and suggested a couple of livening lines, to get the evening underway.

'Nice one Jim,' he said with a smile and we both sort of sensed that we were in for a big night out.

In the public bar, on the wall above the optics, was a huge banner. It was an enlarged photograph of all the locals hanging onto various parts of a transit van. They were all posing in the same t-shirts with the same photograph as the banner.

'What's that all about?' I asked.

Some of the punters at the bar started laughing and Mac chuckled with them.

'Well mate, a bully started to use the pub.'

I knew from schooldays that he didn't tolerate bullies.

'He's a scaffolder, a big lump to be honest and he enjoys picking on people. I like to think of him as an atmosphere thief.'

I was grinning like a Cheshire cat, knowing a decent bit of humour was coming. I also knew that a few tough blokes used the pub and that the scaffolder must be something by size or reputation as he still possessed a full set of teeth. Mac did a fair bit of boxing at school and we had been involved in a number of brawls at football matches and around the various bars when we were in our teens. Now in our twenties, we no longer went to football matches and avoided the dodgier bars.

The scaffolder phoned Mac, a signwriter by trade, and told him he was starting his own business which he was calling Poles & Planks. He left his van in the pub carpark on a Thursday with the relevant art work on the passenger seat. He wanted the van signwritten by Monday. Mac was not about to drop everything for, to use his words, 'that dickhead'. Monday came and went and Tuesday he received a phone call from one very irate scaffolder. He said in no uncertain terms that he was going to be in The Cricks on Friday to pick up the keys and his van better be signwritten.

The signwriting was wonderful; a real piece of artwork. The van was signed with a snakes and ladders theme! Lots of colour and smiling snakes. He also replaced the company name with Snakes & Ladders.

Friday arrived and Mac together with a fair number of the locals were in the bar wearing their t-shirts, banner in place on the wall. The bully walked in, not a happy man, and the pub went silent. He walked straight up to the bar and picked up his keys. He walked out to hoots of derision. A couple of months passed and he hadn't been back. In fact Mac wasn't going to the gym as much as he did after the initial incident, sharpening up in case of any backlash. The coke and hash probably helped but I laughed so much my cheekbones hurt.

After a bit of banter and a few jokes with the other drinkers, we found a corner where we could have some privacy.

'So what's the news, then?' he asked.

I told him that I had signed a contract to work in the Middle East and the reasons why.

'Not a bad shout at all, Mr Payne,' he said.

'We'd better make this weekend a proper celebration then.'

I suggested we take a walk down into the town for a bit of bar hopping. Mac thought this was a good idea but warned we better not go too mental as we were going to a party. I groaned and told him what he already knew. I hated house parties where I didn't really know anyone. He told me to stop whinging. This party would be different and I would know some of the people there. He cut off my questions and told me to show a little patience and to have a little faith.

A lad on his way home offered us a lift into town. He dropped us off at the top of Old Christchurch Road, one of the more lively roads in Bournemouth. As we walked down towards the centre of town, I saw a long queue of men.

'What's that all about?' I asked.

'Oh shit, yeah, I'd forgotten. That's a new lap dancing club recently opened,' was the reply.

'What? In Bournemouth?' I asked.

'Yes, a bit strange, I agree,' said Mac.

'Someone on the council must have been given a huge bung,' I suggested.

Deep in conversation, we crossed the road and walked past the queue. We came to the entrance which featured two doors. The line was waiting outside the door on the left. The door on the right was free so we walked in. Two huge men, clad in evening dress, were in the doorway.

'Evening gentlemen,' said one. 'Can I see your membership cards please?'

Mac told them he wasn't a member yet but wanted to become one.

'No problem, sir,' was the reply. 'If you could just fill out a short form at reception?'

Mac did just that and paid the £10 subscription together with the £5 entrance fee which seemed ridiculously cheap to me, compared to some of the clubs in London that different brokers had taken me to since I started working in the City. I told the receptionist, that I lived in London but was it possible for my friend to sign me in as his guest? This was not a problem so I paid my entrance fee and in we went. All very easy and civilised. I was a bit confused about the long queue.

We sat at the bar and looked at the drinks menu. After ordering a couple of imported bottle beers listed at a ridiculous price, we watched a couple of topless girls gyrating around poles. Two hostesses approached us and offered private lap dances upstairs. We said maybe later as we needed to discuss a bit of business. I ordered more beers and said with a wink and a smile, 'This tab is on me, mate. I'll put it on a card. Seriously anything you want.'

'I'm not really into all this, to be honest,' he said. 'I'm just a bit curious to see what goes on.'

Two more beers arrived and I asked Mac how business was going.

He told me he was visiting France a lot lately and could get as much work as he wanted. He explained that they didn't really do signwriting in Normandy. With a twinkle in his eye he told me how he was working at the docks, on a cherry picker, painting 'Condor Ferries' in enormous letters on the side of a huge ferry. He had painted 'CON' when bad weather closed in. For a day and a half he sat in a nearby bar waiting for the weather to improve. He returned to Bournemouth telling the contractor that he would be back as soon as the wind and rain let up. Back home he got on with work that was backing up. Two weeks later he received an irascible phone call from his French contact. Mac didn't want to drop what he was doing and went into stall tactics. He put on a Welsh accent and pretended to be the accountant. 'Sorry, I don't know where he is at the moment,' he said in a sing-song voice.

The Frenchman was exasperated.

'As you come close to the port you can see the ferry from everywhere. This has been on the local media for a week and has now been in an article in the national newspapers. It was even the funny epilogue that closed the national television news yesterday. Do you know what 'con' means in French? I will tell you, mon cher, it means 'cunt'. Tell your sign writer I need the D – just the D.'

Enjoying a good chuckle we finished our beers and without visiting the 'upstairs' I settled the bill. We trawled a couple of bars and then Mac decided it was time to head off to the party. We caught a taxi to the Southbourne area getting dropped at an off-license where we bought a case of beer and more fags. The party was a short walk away and we could not have missed it: the music was pumping out.

I was amazed. We entered a once functioning hotel which had clearly seen better days. The garden was a little overgrown but still managed to accommodate a range of hammocks, deckchairs, sofas and beanbags with groups of people in various stages of drug- and alcohol-induced intoxication. They were sitting, sprawling, chilling and mostly talking bollocks. As we wandered around the outside of the building, we came across a makeshift bar which was set up in a small lean-to building with cradles for the beer kegs. Quite a lot of people were milling around and the atmosphere was brilliant.

A lot of the party animals were coming up to us, saying hello. I was introduced to some of the guests but just a short time later forgot all their names. Mac spotted the host of the party and introduced him to me. He was another chap who liked to live life to the full, another who believed that 'life is not a dress rehearsal'. Mac attracted mavericks and I always enjoyed meeting them. Our host made decent money from a company he started, a specialist sock retail business. He bought the old hotel and planned to refurbish it, so a party before the work commenced made perfect sense. I reckon a lot of work had gone into setting up for the party.

'Let me show you around. I'll tell you about my plans for the refurb.'

After the tour he headed off to schmooze with his guests.

'Shall we catch up with Graeme?' asked Mac.

'Definitely. I always enjoy seeing Graeme,' I replied.

'He's the DJ, Jim.'

'Since when? I've never heard about this before.'

'Not his regular line of work, I grant you. I think he is doing the host a favour.'

We headed up a cast-iron fire escape attached to the side of the building and there, on a bit of flat roof, was Graeme. He was behind some decks playing music and controlling a light show. The sounds boomed out and people were dancing and generally jigging about.

'It's a rave – best we do another line!' I shouted into Mac's ear.

We walked towards the DJ. Graeme hugged me.

'When did you get down here? Mac kept that one quiet.'

While Graeme passed me a freshly lit joint, I replied, 'Just this afternoon. I'm only here for the weekend.'

I found a bit of space beside all his kit and proceeded to chop up three lines. I snorted a line and passed the rolled-up fiver to Graeme.

'Nice one, Jim. Anything you particularly want to hear?' he asked.

'Anything mate – it's all good.'

I passed Mac the joint and Graeme passed him the fiver. He

snorted the last line, took a huge toke on the joint, exhaled, and, with a smile on his face and a twinkle in his eye, said, 'I knew you would enjoy this. Not your typical party is it?'

The following evening after a couple of lunchtime beers Mac dropped me at my father's house. He lived a dozen or so miles from Bournemouth in the New Forest. My brother Steve was visiting and we all had a good catch up. We went to a Toby Carvery for Sunday lunch and then in the evening Steve and I caught the train to Waterloo.

Back in London I was waiting to go. All the paperwork was in order and I had ticked everything on my 'to-do list'. A phone conversation led to an agreed date of departure and a ticket for Kuwait Airways arrived in the post. I felt a tiny spasm; it was excitement. This was it. I was really going to do this!

3

Settling in Kuwait

Kuwait has a prohibition on alcohol and this includes the national airline. Therefore, I decided that the best place to wait for boarding was the bar. The flight was approximately six and a half hours with a further two hours to add for the time difference. I should be in Kuwait around ten pm. As the journey approached its end, I looked through the window and saw the flares in the oilfields. A short time later the sky was ablaze with the lights of Kuwait city.

As a child I remembered the overwhelming heat on descending the steps to the runway. All these years later I would have to wait until I left the terminal to experience the same feeling because we got off the plane and into arrivals via a gangway; air-conditioning all the way.

Immigration and customs took an age. I later came to realise that this was standard practice. Eventually I walked out of the airport and caught a taxi to my hotel in the city. During check-in, the hotel receptionist informed me that a car was arriving at ten in the morning to take me to the bank. I unpacked, readied everything for the morning, and went to bed where I lay awake, unable to sleep.

The following morning, suited and booted, I entered the restaurant and ordered coffee. A buffet breakfast was on offer. I was greatly disappointed to learn that pork was also forbidden in the country. The sausages and bacon were both beef. The sausages were very average and the bacon horrible. I am not a pork junkie but I do like a cooked breakfast when staying in a hotel and so this was not a great start to the day.

I was finishing a second cup of coffee when a driver from the bank sent a message to say he was in reception. A quarter of an hour later we walked into the head office of The MBME bank. Treasury took up the whole of the third floor and the driver used an entry key letting me into the dealing room.

I couldn't believe how quiet the room was, certainly not what I was used to in the City of London. There were several desks dotted around the room responsible for precious metals, investments, money markets and customers. The desk with the squawk boxes (open lines to brokers), which were constantly calling the prices of the major currencies, was making the most noise, and was instantly recognisable as the foreign exchange desk. This was where I would be sitting.

It sat eight or so men, a mix of pinkies (a term used to describe Westerners in the Middle East), locals and Indians. They were all staring at me. A Danish chap in his mid-forties stood up, came over and shook my hand.

'Hello, you must be James. My name is Steen and I am the chief dealer. Mr Shadid is out of the bank for a while, so please come and meet your new colleagues.'

'Nice to meet you,' I replied, 'but please call me Jim.'

We took a quick tour of the other desks where I met, and

promptly forgot, the other dealers' names. Steen showed me my seat and once I was settled, he introduced me to the guys who worked on the Forex desk. Some hours later Mr Shadid came into the room and, after exchanging pleasantries, disappeared into his office.

The following weeks were a hive of activity. There were a lot of personnel issues to take care of. Firstly there was the residency permit involving a chest x-ray and reams of paperwork; these submissions were by the kilogram. I imagined a man sitting behind a counter with a set of scales on which applications were placed. After a quick look he would send you on your way to find another kilo or two. This applied to all applications. Next was a Kuwaiti driving license, unobtainable until you acquired residency. This, too, involved clearing a few acres of woodland, turning it into paper and after processing, placing it onto the scales. Always, always have a few hundred passport-sized photos in reserve – they do love a photo!

The other pressing issue was accommodation. Human Resources sent a Mr Bakir to meet me and every few days he took me to look at various properties. I settled on an apartment very close to the Gulf Street which, as the name implies, followed the coastline. It was next to the Crown Prince Palace in the Shaab district.

Unlike the personnel issues which I took in my stride, adapting my trading style was a much harder adjustment. In the City I quoted customers and other banks and then covered whatever position resulted. The brokers shouted prices and you could hear the buying and selling. News was constantly being updated. Information on large orders, either to buy or sell, filtered through and this engendered a feel for the market.

The dealing room turned out to be even quieter than that first day. I was lulled into a false impression by the activity which proved to be unusual. The normal atmosphere was akin to a pin dropping. Customer activity was very small and the other banks mainly called into the major centres. Occasionally we made a market before London opening but, in practice, the markets were usually at a lull waiting for the City.

The brokers generally left you alone unless you rattled their cage. For example, if you asked for a price on cable (GBP against USD) they started quoting and kept updating with prices in the hope of picking up some business. The broker received £11 for every million dealt from both the buyer and the seller. As we generally traded in amounts of five million, their potential commission was £110 every time a deal was done. Brokers sat in close proximity around a desk and each served several banks. For instance, if a dealer wanted to buy, they placed a bid or took the offer.

A couple of months passed by and I lost money consistently; nothing too dramatic but enough to be a worry. The banks in the Middle East like to employ foreign exchange dealers trained in the major centres and then whisk them away to an alien trading environment. Being able to adapt and change was essential if I was to survive in the desert.

In foreign exchange there are two approaches to analysing the market and most successful dealers use a combination of both. The fundamental approach considers the economic relationship between two countries with dealers attempting to predict the value of one currency against the other. For example, the release of figures such as jobless claims are useful as an indication of whether one currency is undervalued against the other and like wildcards in a game of poker, the release of economic data can give the markets a mad few hours if they do not come out as expected.

Technical analysis, or charting, has a completely different approach. Charts are graphs that plot price action over a period of time, the main tenet being price action discounts everything. They are useful in identifying the market environment whether the market is trending up or down or if it is trendless. Once the market environment has been identified, the chart is extremely useful in knowing when, and at what level, to take a position and then when to take profits or cut losses.

I realised that trading by the 'seat of my pants' was not an option so over the coming weeks I spent my time learning all aspects of technical analysis. I concluded that the best way to make profits was to identify a trend, follow it and hope for a decent movement in the market. Building currency positions happened over days or weeks, very different to the intraday dealing I was used to.

During my first week I received a phone call from Steve who worked for a broking company. He introduced himself and welcomed me to the country. After a good chinwag, he invited me to his home in order to meet some of the other 'pinkies' who worked in the market. He picked me up from my hotel.

'Hi Jim. I bet you're gagging for a beer.'

'Abso-bloody-lutely,' I replied.

He laughed and off we drove. A short while later I was standing at a bar in his home with a bunch of other expats enjoying a homemade beer. Everyone made me feel welcome and gave me a myriad of advice. By the end of the evening, amongst other things, I knew where to go to buy a car and how to put a brew on – and I don't mean tea!

Life became easier once I moved into an apartment close to the Crown Prince's palace and bought a car. Firstly I went to a large supermarket and arrived at the checkout with a couple of trolleys. There were ten cases of near beer (non-alcoholic: Barbican and Buckler being examples), ten cartons each of grape and apple juice, twenty kilos of sugar, plastic tubing, Milton's (a cleaning fluid for babies' bottles) and various other items. The lad on the checkout said, 'You have forgotten the yeast, sir.'

A quick dash to baking aids took care of that.

My social life revolved entirely around the banking and broking community – something that needed to be addressed. Lovely people, but they tended to talk about the markets in the main. Things took a turn for the better after I drove into the back of another car. A tall Englishman got out of the car in front and I did the same trying to look contrite.

'I am so sorry, mate. I'm fairly new to the country. I was trying to work out where I should be going and lost concentration.'

It was just a little shunt but there was some damage to his bumper.

'Don't worry, these things happen,' he said magnanimously. 'Unfortunately we have to go to the local police station to get an incident number. Insurance won't process a claim without one.'

We drove to the police station where no one spoke English. We gathered from a mix of broken Arabic and charades that we were required to wait for a particular officer.

While we were waiting, Keith, a loss adjuster, and I got acquainted. I liked him and over time we became good friends. He mentioned that he was a bit worried as he had been at the beach all day and had several drinks inside him. I reassured him that he appeared completely sober and I couldn't smell any alcohol on him. I also hinted that I could do with a drink myself and he said we could go for a couple once we were given our incident number.

The officer arrived and after booking the incident, told me I was fined fifty dinars (roughly one hundred pounds) as I had admitted liability. I only had thirty dinars on me and quick as a flash, Keith took twenty dinars out of his pocket. The policeman was completely baffled. He told us that he did not understand the English. We were both smiling,

'You,' he said pointing at me, 'drove into the back of his car', he pointed at Keith. 'Now you are lending him money to pay the fine.'

I got the feeling he thought we should be shouting insults at each other.

After following Keith for around twenty minutes, we arrived at a small apartment complex. I was amazed when we entered a flat that was converted into an English-style pub. Keith introduced me to Mike, a building contractor, the creator of this marvellous place.

'Welcome to The Glue Pot, Jim.'

The Glue Pot was aptly named as you popped in for a quick one and then got stuck. The people who used this bar and called themselves Potters became my good friends. They had various jobs, none of them in banking. Mike told me that if his car was parked facing the wall he was open. In all the time I lived in

Kuwait I never saw his car parked in any other position than open.

The Glue Pot along with the other bars I frequented, including mine, were all free. They worked because the people who used them all contributed. Bachelors brewed or brought cases of 'near beer', soft drinks, bags of ice, etc. Couples invited people to dinner and threw parties. I loved the social life but it only worked because everyone made an effort. Following the fortunate car crash, my social life improved considerably.

When brewing, baker's yeast dies as the alcohol content reaches eighteen per cent. A popular drink at the time was a pint glass filled two-thirds with homemade wine and one third with 7Up. Often you heard the shout from whoever was working the bar, 'Fat or skinny?'

This was to determine whether the punter wanted diet or full fat 7Up. Beer was always favourite when available; again it brewed out at eighteen per cent. We decanted a bottle of beer into a jug and added a can of 'near beer' which also added bubbles and brought the brew to a reasonable strength. I once went to a party that had plenty of brewed beer but no near beer. The place resembled a zoo by 11pm – people jousting with pool cues and other high jinks.

There was also a black market where you could buy Johnnie Walker whisky but always at a big price. Ethanol was cheap and readily available. People mixed it with all sorts to imitate different spirits and liqueurs. Mostly they just mixed it one part Eth to two parts water to make a spirit resembling Vodka. It was not too long before I built a bar. To be honest, I laboured for a friend, Kevin, who did most of the work. Hurrah! I was into the swing of things with a great circle of friends.

Once ingrained into the social life, I tried to repay the many kindnesses shown me when I first arrived. I made an effort to help newcomers and only once did I regret giving up my time. I took a newly arrived couple to various places furniture shopping. Then I took them to the supermarket, bought all the necessary and put their first brew on for them. It was the only time I set foot in their apartment. I was on bachelor status and used to love it when a couple or family invited me to eat with them. This couple drank in my bar four or five times and I still hadn't been asked to theirs, not even to taste the beer I brewed for them. Goodness knows I dropped enough hints about how the beer had turned out! I stopped inviting them and hardly ever saw them again as others also decided they weren't worth the effort. They were silly because it only took a small effort to secure a great social life.

4

Marriage & the Fifty Club

Mandy and I were speaking on the telephone regularly and she was due to arrive at the airport. A friend arranged a visit visa for her under the premise she was his wife's cousin. Couples needed to be married in order to cohabit and we arranged an appointment at the ministries complex in order to 'plight our troth'.

Believing this to be just a formality, I was dressed fairly casually in a pair of trousers together with a shirt and tie. Steve and Beth who were to be our witnesses were also dressed inconspicuously. Mandy however, was in a wedding dress she brought with her from the UK.

The official was shocked and a little uncertain as to what to do. He decided we were not breaking any rules and with a big grin said, 'Welcome my dears.'

The workers at the ministry, particularly the young women, were soon crowding the corridor trying to get a glimpse of the mad Englishwoman.

We returned to our apartment with Steve and Beth. Everyone I met and liked popped round and a jolly drinks party ensued.

Mandy and I fell into an expat way of life and were mostly happy. One year later, Charlotte, our beautiful daughter, was born. I was starting to feel a bit like a grown up. I was the head of a family, lived in a nice apartment and worked in a decent job.

One Monday morning I was sitting at the desk when the squawk box from a broker started calling for Jim. I clicked in, 'What do you want, Sean?'

'Good morning, Jim. How are you today?'

'It's Monday morning, you tool. What do you want?' I enquired.

Sean was laughing. 'I have decided to start The Fifty Club,' he said.

He had my attention.

'Righto! I'll bite – what's the Fifty Club?' I asked.

Sean said he would call me on the outside unrecorded line and clicked out. He explained that anyone who did fifty million dollars' worth of business with him during the week could come round to his on Friday after work and drink Johnnie Walker whisky. I told him I thought it was an excellent idea and closed down the call.

Dealers can deal direct with other banks or through one of the different broking companies. I thought bribing the local market with alcohol was an inspired idea. Always alert to a bit of market humour, a smile came onto my face. The market was a little bullish and the offers were being paid leading to the market drifting a little higher.

I clicked into Sean's box. 'Get me a dollar mark [US dollar against deutschemark] in twenty-five million please.'

In the broking market five million was a standard amount

and the amount most commonly traded. Twenty-five million was unusual. I guessed Sean might be wondering whether I was winding him up. He called his London link and got a price.

'Mine!' I shouted as I took the offer.

The market moved a little higher. This was very good and in no time it was about fifteen points higher. I clicked into the box again. 'Sean, another dollar mark in twenty-five please.'

Within ten seconds he quoted a price from London and they read me as a buyer due to my previous trade. I hit the bid and closed out my position. The position from start to finish took just a few minutes and I made a little over twenty thousand dollars profit. Sean came on the box and gave me the names of the banks I had dealt with.

'Cheers pal, I'll see you Friday,' I said and turned his box off.

The other forex traders on my desk were all pissing themselves. Friday evening I walked into Sean's villa and made my way to his bar. There were eight traders clearly in good spirits. I accepted the cat calls and hoots of derision with good grace. Sean had already told them of my two-deal entry to The Fifty Club followed by turning his box off. The humour appealed to them. Sean placed a fresh bottle of Johnnie Walker Red Label in front of me. I took the cap off and threw it over my shoulder.

'We won't be needing that again,' I said to more laughter.

The evening was proving to be most enjoyable. The company was good and the whisky was flowing. I had read an article about potential German unification and at that time the East German ostmark was trading against the West German deutschemark at ten to one on the black market. I believed that unification was closer than imagined and may take place within a few years. Germany was likely to exchange at no more than two to one. My reason being that Germany could not erode pensions, house values, etc and create second-class citizens of the East Germans. I started a debate. Adrian, a dealer I respected, thought I was onto something whereas the others thought I must be on drugs.

'We should all go to Berlin and buy a load of Ostmarks on the black market and when they reunify we'll be quids in,' I said.

'What are you going to do with these Ostmarks while you wait for this reunification, if and when it ever happens?' asked one of the sceptics.

'Put 'em in a bloody drawer,' said Adrian a little loudly.

Whisky is never a great idea when debating.

Four months later the wall came down and Germany reunified with an exchange rate of one to one. It must have cost them fortunes. This was perhaps the greatest call I ever made during my career as a currency trader and I missed it. In fairness I hadn't returned to Europe during that time and I never expected a united Germany to emerge so quickly.

The debate petered out when Charles entered the bar. There was a respectful lull as he said hello to those of us he knew and was introduced to the others by Sean. Charles worked for the Bank of England (hence the little bit of respect) and was on secondment as an advisor to the Governor of The Central Bank of Kuwait. I liked him: he was intelligent and witty, a winning combination.

'I've just had the best laugh in years,' he said with a beaming grin.

'What's that then?' asked Sean.

Charles told us that the Governor wanted to know the average price of oil for the coming year and asked him to arrange a conference with various experts. The meeting had just concluded and he was still buzzing.

At a huge cost, he arranged for two experts from the oil industry, a couple of economists specialising in the oil market and two representatives from the Bank of England, to attend. There were twelve in attendance, the six mentioned along with Charles, the Governor and four up and coming Kuwaiti lads, employees of the Kuwait Central Bank. After a general opening from the Governor, he asked one of the Bank of England representatives to give his view. The following took place: 'I assume we are all in agreement that world interest rates will remain low for quite a considerable time,' he said.

A voice rang out – a young Kuwaiti who should have been listening instead of talking, 'What do you mean assume? What if ... what if ... ' he spluttered.

The eyes of the room were on him.

'What if, for example, Kennedy did not get killed, but the Russian one did?'

The meeting room was silent. Time seemed to stand still. Without batting an eyelid the brain from the Bank of England said, 'I am not sure the point you are trying to make, young man, but if you are asking me what repercussions might have resulted and how it could have affected world affairs, if John F. Kennedy was not shot on the 22 November 1963 in Dallas, Texas but Nikita Khrushchev was assassinated instead, I cannot possibly give you an answer. I can however and with all certainty tell you that Aristotle Onassis would not have married Mrs Khrushchev.'

There were a few suppressed chortles and guffaws and the

Governor, with a smile on his face, called for a twenty minute break. Needless to say when the session resumed, the young man was not present. We fell about laughing, not only for the wit, but we could all relate as we saw young men from wealthy and powerful families in our dealing rooms who didn't really have the wherewithal to be there.

I built a nice life for myself in the desert. Money was good and the social scene fabulous. There was a good night to be had whenever you wanted. As far as work was concerned things were just fine as well. Time passed with employees leaving the bank for various reasons and new guys joining. Mr John Henry, the new treasurer, appointed me chief dealer. The work became a lot more exciting because I was running the room as well as working closely with John. There was a fair amount of travel, all first class, and I was loving it. One particular week stands out in my memory as being of note. The week ended with a trip to Bahrain; various chaps, bankers, brokers, friends all ready to let loose.

The week began as many others. I was drinking my first cup of coffee when Majid came into the room in a stressed state. He was the senior of two lads who were working for me in the private lounge. They were behind a Perspex screen in a booth within the lounge. Through squawk boxes the two lads fed prices to a few extremely rich businessmen who sat in the lounge drinking tea and accessing the news channels, charts, etc. They speculated with their own vast funds.

'I want to resign, Mr Jim,' said Majid. He was shaking with rage.

'No you don't. Let's go into the conference room for a chat.'

'Majid will now be referee of the room.'

The Arabs love their football and there were a few grins.

'A yellow card bans you from the room for a week, a red card for a month.'

There was laughing now and the atmosphere in the room had turned turtle.

'Listen gentlemen, I want you to make money but please don't give the guys a hard time if you get it wrong.'

We left the lounge. Majid had to enter his booth from another door. Before I went back to the dealing room, I asked him if he was ok.

'Very happy, Mr Jim. I think it will be ok now.'

5

Bedouin Tribesmen

I was half way through the *Kuwait Times* crossword when a Westerner entered the dealing room – my guess was British given his ghostly pallor. This man brought great amusement because he was dressed like a Kuwaiti. He was called into the treasurer's office and I can only imagine the conversation – something along the lines of 'go home and change into a suit, you bloody idiot!' An hour later I was introduced to an appropriately suited Khalid Al-Rhodos who, prior to his conversion to Islam, had been Brian James.

He was Oxbridge educated and, like some people with superior intelligence, just a little bit eccentric. Whether mismanagement by human resources or a bizarre joke, he sat on the customer desk. He should have been hidden away in his own office working on analysis and the formulation of trading strategies. This might have been more productive as opposed to pissing off customers.

He seemed to enjoy confrontation which made him unpopular. In fact I never saw him socially outside the bank. I have friends who converted to Islam for the purposes of marrying Arab women. Once the ceremony was completed however, they reverted to their Christian names with their Muslim name only used by friends wanting to pull their leg. My new colleague converted for his own reasons, presumably religious, and only responded to his Islamic name which was a concoction from his love of Rhodes.

Khalid excelled himself on a few occasions. For example, he had only spoken in a professional capacity to a Bahraini woman working for Reuters, when he decided to visit her place of work, get on his knees and propose, much to the amusement and embarrassment of all her colleagues.

On another occasion Khalid limped very gingerly into the dealing room after being absent for a few days. Marc, a colleague from my desk, was sniggering.

'Come on, Marc, let us into the secret. What's so funny?' I asked.

He had already had a confrontation with Khalid and was chortling when he replied, 'He was beaten on his feet at the police station!'

Most expats chose to live in apartments or villas. Khalid, however, decided to live at the Sheraton Hotel, which was the designated venue for an Organisation of Petroleum Exporting Countries (OPEC) meeting. Security was on high alert and everyone coming or going was subject to scrutiny. He was returning from work when a police sergeant asked him to open his briefcase. He refused on principle and, after an undignified tussle, was carted off to face his punishment.

Unlike the rest of the country's workforce whose weekend was Thursday afternoon and Friday, we worked a standard Monday to Friday with Saturday and Sunday off in line with the international markets. Occasionally we sloped off around lunchtime on a Friday and enjoyed a weekend away in Bahrain or Dubai. These were very heavy drinking affairs where we met up with bankers, brokers and various other drinking companions. To coin a phrase we 'got on it!'

I loved my trips away and always returned with sore cheekbones from laughing and a hangover from hell. Having been in the Middle East for a few years now, I knew a fair amount of pissheads living in these alcohol oases and they were very accommodating, literally putting us up and putting up with us. I was usually claimed by Ronnie or Reggie, the latter an amazing maverick of a man with a voracious thirst. Both big men, they worked in the same dealing room. Dressing alike in black trousers, white shirts and black Dr Marten shoes, had earned them their nicknames.

Alcohol was permitted to non-Muslims in the hotels and private clubs and there were plenty of excellent bars and nightclubs dotted around both centres.

Friday eventually came around, 'Hurrah!', and I met with friends at the airport around lunchtime. We were on the Gulf Air flight and were being picked up from Bahrain Airport to be whisked away on a non-stop, booze-fuelled weekend.

Being summer, most of the wives and children returned to Europe for the long school holiday, avoiding the fierce temperatures. The seats on the plane were mostly filled with male expats. These guys were in small parties from various sports and social clubs and other small groups, aged roughly twenty-five to fifty, all with the common purpose of losing brain cells.

Gulf Air is the national carrier of Bahrain and, as such, serves alcohol. Most of the passengers hadn't tasted a real beer in quite some time and so, as soon as the seatbelt sign was turned off, the air stewardesses worked like crazy to make sure everyone got a drink. One flight I was on they were literally throwing cases of lager at us and we collected the money from the various passengers, paid the air crew and distributed the beers ourselves.

This flight was an up and down affair taking less than an hour. I, like the others, got through three or four cans. The record was a ridiculous amount of cans and miniature whiskies but I knew it was going to be a long night and so tried to pace myself.

On this particular journey there was an old boy who ordered a beer and just as the stewardess was about to pour it for him, she lost her balance in a bit of turbulence and the contents ended up in his lap. The distraught attendant, apologising profusely, ran to the galley and returned with a tea towel. She started to rub around his crotch area in an attempt to dry him off. It started with Adrian shouting: 'Hey! Hey!' and pouring the remains of his can into his own lap. He then shouted, 'Me next, love.'

We were all in hysterics and to a chorus of 'Hey! Hey!' we all followed suit. These Gulf Air stewardesses had experienced all these sorts of high jinks before and she took it all in good spirits.

The flight landed and we cleared customs and border control with no hitches. As a large body of men with wet crotches we all made our way to the arrivals hall. I overheard two Brits who were clearly waiting for someone, having a bit of a conversation.

'Shit, that must have been quite a flight,' said the first chap.

The second responded, 'What do you reckon – turbulence?'

Our party was met by two of the lads with large four-wheel drives. These also doubled up as golf carts when used on the sand course – I kid you not. After dropping our bags we made our way to Henry's Bar. We had just missed the 'Who's got the most horrible arse competition?' which was a blessing. Ron, Reg, Mauser, Tom and a few of the others had been in the pub since opening time and were in high spirits. They had all dropped their trousers but Tom was declared the winner and promptly nicknamed 'Tom Perignon'.

The evening became a bit of a blur and I awoke the next morning with a hangover and PDD (Post Drunk Depression). Reg and Susan made bacon sandwiches and a pot of coffee. They both assured me that I hadn't behaved badly the previous evening and so there were no apologies required. Reg asked how I could have insulted anyone when I was incapable of stringing a sentence together! A fair point.

The plan was to spend the day at the Bankers' Club where there was a decent-sized swimming pool and good facilities. We arrived early afternoon and, not being one to sit around outside, I grabbed a Guinness and headed for the snooker room. Some of the lads joined me and time passed. Before I knew it Reg and I were outside the Rugby Club at three am. We could have been in the desert as there was not a soul in sight. Reg put both hands in the air and shouted, 'Last man standing again!'

We arranged an early evening return flight to Kuwait. This gave us plenty of time to enjoy a lunch at Chico's, an Italian restaurant, much favoured by the expat community. By the time I left the Middle East, Sunday lunch at Chico's was a tradition.

The boys from a well-known broking house invited us and having been to lunch with them before, I believed I was prepared for what was to come. I clearly wasn't, and the lunch turned into a memorable debacle following various drinking games.

We left Chico's in a right old state and only just caught our flight. Once back at home, I lay on the sofa wondering how I could possibly be ready for work in the morning. I received absolutely no sympathy from the wife.

Back in the room the following Friday, I checked with Sean regarding The Fifty Club. He assured me his bar was ready to be in full flow that evening. When I arrived John was propping the bar up and waxing lyrical to all the other drinkers.

'There was a hoo-ha in the banking hall today,' he said.

He had heard shouting and saw some scuffling at the main doors to the bank so he headed towards the disturbance. Outside were a group of Bedouin tribesmen, some armed with rifles arguing with various bank employees. Two very nervous armed guards of the bank were barring their entry. A manager from the retail banking sector quickly brought him up to speed.

From time to time there were disputes between the tribes and things could get pretty nasty. During these conflicts the tribes often brought their cash into the various banks and deposited it until things were resolved and life returned to normal. The Bedouins outside carried a large chest and were determined to bring it into the bank but the problem was the various weaponry they were carrying.

John really let rip. 'Quiet!' he screamed.

It achieved the desired effect as everyone shut up. John talked through the manager who translated for him. He informed them that if the chief and a few of his cohorts wanted to come into the bank, then he would do his best to accommodate them. However, there was no way all of them were coming in and certainly, 'No Guns!'

The chief and two of the tribesmen carried the chest straight through to an office adjacent to the main banking hall. John and the manager sat in the office with them and waited for the obligatory tea. Once the customary formalities were out of the way and due procedure observed, they got down to business.

The chest was opened and John was speechless for a moment or two. There was every major currency under the sun – Swiss francs, British pounds, US dollars and other European bank notes together with all the different denominations from around the Middle East and the sub-continent. In total there were millions.

Kuwait became independent in 1961 and the official currency was the dinar. Prior to that in the 1950s, various coins and notes were issued which were no longer legal tender. There were Kuwaiti Paisas, Gulf Rupees and others which fell into that category. The tellers removed all of the redundant monies which they bagged up and returned, apologising for not being able to take them. As for the rest, it was agreed that the monies would be counted by hand and then by machine. When matched, the totals would be agreed with the chief and deposited in the bank.

John left the manager to arrange for the counting and complete the paperwork. He said his protracted goodbyes and headed back to the lifts. This was not to be the end of the matter.

6
Buying Some Gold

Reg called the bank fairly early on the Monday morning and we sallied a few laughs reminiscing the highlights of the weekend.

'I wanted to remind you about Dubai next month, Jim,' he said.

My mind recalled a boozy conversation regarding the upcoming BBBGS (Bahrain Banks and Brokers Golf Society) tournament. This was held annually in Dubai and I promised Reg that I would be there. As he was in the process of moving to Dubai, he offered to put me up.

That year's big sponsor was Reuters and, like most of the dealers in Kuwait, I had a very mixed relationship with them. Reuters had begun life as a news service but, since working in dealing rooms, I had witnessed their explosive growth in the banking sector. They introduced a direct dealing system much to the chagrin of the broking companies. This allowed the dealer to contact any bank in the world, ask for a price and deal directly using a four-letter code. They provided a charting service along with a decent news feed and we all relied on

Reuters more and more as a tool of the trade.

Reuters always suffered problems with the Ministry of Communications on a Friday. As I have mentioned, the working week was Saturday to Thursday lunchtime and, as such, most workers didn't give a fig if the communications system crashed on a Friday. The only people who got upset by these crashes were the currency traders who ploughed on with no news or chart service and no direct dealer. I called Reuters occasionally, whinging and moaning, but was always given the same excuse: 'The problem is at the Ministry and no one is working there today.' Eventually, I marked down the times that we did not receive a service and docked their monthly bill accordingly. This made me unpopular amongst the Reuters hierarchy but eventually they accepted it with good grace.

My trip to Dubai was all organised. I phoned some of my dealing and broking friends and arranged to meet up. I let slip to a pal who enjoyed a smoke that I was bringing a bit of pot with me. I was not in the habit of indulging while in the Middle East but now and then a piece came my way. Airport security was very different in those days and so I was not particularly worried when I hid the offending article in my underpants. My pot-loving friend offered to send the company car and driver to collect me from the airport and take me to The George and Dragon where we were all meeting up.

When I was a young child during the 1960s, I saw a movie where the hero was met at an airport by a limousine driver with a name board. This seemed glamorous and sophisticated to me and, since then, I had harboured a fantasy to be met in such a manner. Walking into the arrivals hall I spotted a man with a name board. JIM THE JUNKIE it announced to all and sundry. My fantasy was fulfilled and shattered all at the same time. How very funny, ha bloody ha! I laughed all the way to the pub. I walked into the bar and the conversation temporarily halted. My pal asked if the car met me all right.

'Yes thanks, highly bloody whimsical!' I replied and the crowd burst into laughter. The weekend had begun. I gravitated towards Reg and we started to enjoy some bar time. The barman passed him the phone from behind the bar, mobiles still being fairly rare in those days. After a short conversation Reg said, 'Drink up, mate, we have to go.'

We were in a cab on the way to his flat.

'It's all kicking off big time and Mo, my house boy, is starting to panic,' he said.

A few of the lads had gone around to Reg's and, finding that neither he nor Susan were at home, decided to sit at his bar, have a drink and wait. After some time they started to get boisterous.

Reg said, 'Mo reckons the thin one with long hair – '

'Mauser!'

' – Exactly! Well he is doing his Mick Jagger impression, strutting up and down the lounge, using a bar tray as a tambourine. There is an arm-wrestling competition getting out of hand at the bar. Someone is practicing his golf swing in the hallway and Thacker is standing on his head trying to demonstrate a sexual position that no one is interested in.'

Once in the lift, we could hear the music going full blast and so we joined the bedlam.

After rounding up the troops, we went off on a pub crawl and met up with Susan and her friends. People drifted off and others joined, and towards the end of the evening we were in a bar close to Reg and Susan's flat. We had been drinking for six or seven hours now but Reg had disappeared. Knowing his fondness for being 'last man standing', I wondered where he was. Susan asked the crowd back to hers for a drink and off we all went.

Walking into the flat, I burst into laughter. Reg was sporting a pair of budgie smugglers and a pair of Ray Bans. He was sitting in a deck chair with a large beach umbrella shading him from spotlights. He had replaced the rugs from his marble floor with newspapers that were covered in Kentucky Fried Chicken. There was enough food for thirty people.

'Welcome to my BBQ!' he shouted.

Within five minutes Reg twirled the umbrella in front of him and gave his rendition of the classic stripper music – Da Na Na Na! ... Na Na Na Na Na! His budgie smugglers flew across the room and the umbrella rolled to one side. Reg, now completely naked, proceeded to body surf his impromptu BBQ. Things degenerated from there and in the morning, feeling a bit the worse for wear, we made our way to the Dubai Creek golf club. I felt that, today, I was not going to record any sort of a score whatsoever.

The weekend closed with a dinner and prize-giving. Everyone was in a jolly mood, as the booze continued to flow. The CEO of Reuters gave out the prizes and then launched into his speech. He decided to open with some wit, a good idea, and one that is probably recommended in books on public speaking.

'We have seen some good golf this weekend but next year we will see some truly wonderful golf. You see, I have the boffins in the research department developing a club that will perfectly dissect the fairway. The club will centre on the green and all chips will fall within two feet of the hole. When putting, the club will zero in on the hole and the ball cannot miss.'

Some wag from the back shouted, 'But will it work on a Friday?'

The whole room erupted into laughter and it was quite some time before he could continue with his speech.

Jim receiving the Most Improved Player Prize at the BBBGS dinner.

A week or so after my weekend away, I was in John's office for our regular Monday morning meeting. He told me that the Bedouins returned while I was in Dubai. They walked into the banking hall and asked for their money back. John, realising that their skirmish was probably at an end, still hoped he might convince them to leave their money where it was. They were not interested. They just wanted their cash back which they would no doubt box up and bury in the desert again. Realising he wasn't going to change the old chief's mind, he asked the cashiers to close their accounts and return their deposits. A short while later he was called down to the main banking hall again. In a small private office the Bedouin chief looked angry.

'Where is my money?'

John looked at the cash laid out on the table in different denominations and looked a bit perplexed.

'This is your money.' John pointed at the amassed fortune.

The nomad shook his head. 'That is not my money!'

He pulled an A4 size pad out of a bag he carried with him and flipped it open. Each page was covered in bank note serial numbers. He pointed to the cash. 'That is not my money. I want my money.'

John spent an hour or so trying to explain modern banking. He told the customer his money was now floating around the economy and it was impossible to give him back the exact same notes he had deposited. He explained the cash on the table was perfectly legal tender and if he wanted his money back it was that or nothing. The chief was definitely not happy, mainly because all the new serial numbers needed writing in a new pad. We both sat a bit bemused before we returned to the order of the day and completed our meeting.

Towards the end of the week, I wanted more volatility in the markets and more activity. I was bored and wanted some action. On the Thursday I got what I wanted. I sensed there was something brewing on the metals desk. Usama approached me and asked if I could make a price on gold to a customer.

'Usama, you guys are the experts. Why can't you quote?'

'Mr Jim, we can only quote up to a certain amount and this exceeds it. You'll have to quote him. You're the only one here with a big enough limit.'

Good – some action at last! I was fed up with sitting on my hands. Feeling the tingle of adrenalin, I checked the gold price.

The standard gold bar, held as gold reserves by central banks and traded amongst bullion dealers, is 12.4 kg, equivalent to 400 troy ounces. A usual trade between dealers being 5,000 ounces. So when the customer wanted a quote in 3,720 kg, which by my reckoning was 300 bars, a very specific amount, I reckoned he was a seller. Usama gave me his view and agreed. I asked how easily it could be covered in the market place and whether our selling would have any effect on price. I also asked how stable the market was and what the short-term outlook might be. Finally, I suggested quoting a very low price, hoping above all hope that he was indeed a seller. Usama agreed and my bid was around US$46 million and, sure enough, he sold to us.

The metals desk immediately buzzed about getting prices and we managed to cover the full amount, in the region of 120,000 ounces, before the market moved. A quick estimation and I knew that we had made an extremely handsome profit. I was well pleased and congratulated the guys.

I was blissfully ignorant that anything was wrong until a very worried Usama asked me to accompany him to the main banking hall. The customer was waiting and asked us to follow him outside. He took us to his flat-bed truck where more than four tons of gold was sitting on a pallet.

'Usama! What on earth ... ?'

I was speechless for a moment. I just stared at the gold and then at the two armed gentlemen who guarded the truck.

Gold tends to just sit in a bonded warehouse in Switzerland, or so I thought. I had never heard of anyone actually taking delivery of the precious metal.

It all worked out in the end. We had to have the gold couriered under armed guard, at great expense. The precious metal was assayed and bonded at more cost, meaning a large part of the profit was wiped out but, as they say, you live and learn.

It was during a party when I first heard rumblings of discord between Iraq and Kuwait. Following an OPEC meeting, a rumour arose. Delegates from both countries had supposedly taken to throwing their food at each other during a lunch. Clearly they were not hungry! A general conversation developed with several of the guests all trying to pontificate at the same time. I gathered the following from the ensuing cacophony.

The Iran-Iraq war which finished in 1988 left Iraq's economy crippled. The breakdown meant that they were unable to repay the loan incurred to Kuwait. The debt in excess of $10 billion should therefore be forgiven. After all, the war also benefited Kuwait as well!

Iraq argued that Kuwait was guilty of lateral drilling beneath the borderline, essentially stealing oil from their fields, particularly the Rumaila field, to the tune of $2.4 billion. They argued that their neighbours were lowering the price of oil, ignoring OPEC production quotas, manipulating their currency and, in general, of being poor neighbours. Finally, their argument was historic – that Kuwait was the nineteenth province of Iraq. The Kuwaitis disagreed. Whilst their arguments swirled in the mists of time, the truth that Kuwait was a British Protectorate until they gained independence in 1961, seemed most relevant to me.

This creation of a state with an Emir was strongly objected to by the Iraq government. In fact, they planned an invasion at that time which was prevented by the Arab League. Kuwait became a member of the United Nations (UN) in 1963 which gave credibility and ratification to their independence. There have been many tensions and arguments between them since those times. This was, so they tell me, mostly the fault of British Colonialism! I think Saddam just saw a big fat plum, ripe for the picking.

My three-year contract was coming to an end and talks with the bank regarding renewal were still ongoing. After discussing things with Mandy, I decided not to renew. All conversations at work and socially were about the building tensions in the area and so I convinced Mandy to take our daughter Charlotte and return home. I hoped to wrap things up, selling the cars and shipping the furniture before I also returned to the UK.

She was keen for me to return with them but I told her I wanted her to get everything ready at our flat in London. I pointed out that I was still under contract and wasn't going to jeopardise my end of contract bonus.

I said, 'You know what they're like. They will be threatening and posturing for months.'

Fortunately Mandy and Charlotte were safely back in the UK when Saddam Hussein turned up the heat and put 250,000 Republican Guard (Elite Iraqi troops) on the border. The summer was upon us and with temperatures exceeding fifty degrees centigrade on occasions, you could fry an egg on a spade if it was left in the sun. I knew that no one in their right mind would invade now. He would not give up the opportunity to posture and threaten. No – end of September, possibly October at the very earliest, and I hoped to be long gone by then.

Although it was obvious that these troops were an offensive

rather than defensive force, I still believed I had plenty of time to leave the country. The next day – 1 August 1990 – I walked into John's office and told him I would not be renewing my contract when it expired on 6 September.

John is a wonderfully decent man. 'Look Jim, you might as well make today your last day. Organise your shipping and I will push personnel for your end of term benefits.'

He told me not to worry about my cars too much as they could be sold after I left the country. I drank a skinful that night and went to bed feeling glad with the way things were working out.

7

The Invasion Begins

The next day, 2 August 1990, Iraqi tanks rolled down the Gulf Street. Iraqi troops walked behind firing indiscriminately. A helicopter gunship hovered over the Dasman Palace. The date became firmly engrained in my psyche, as familiar a date as my own birthday. I was awoken by a cacophony of sound. There was the most horrendous roaring din outside and the phone was ringing. I was still half asleep, befuddled by the previous night's celebration. I staggered across the lounge in my underpants and picked up the noisy instrument.

'Um ... hello,' I mumbled.

'Hello yourself,' came the reply. 'Do you know there is an invasion going on?'

'Hi Martin – just woken up and don't know too much about anything at the moment.'

'Don't go anywhere chief. I'm coming right over.'

I went back in the bedroom and quickly pulled on shorts, t-shirt and flip-flops and ventured outside. Samir, the farash (handyman/gardener), was watering the plants in the beds surrounding the compound.

I liked Samir and his family. He was Iraqi but had been resident in Kuwait for over a decade. When his brother-in-law died in the Iran-Iraq war, his sister and her children came to live with him. He and his wife had young children of their own and so, while I knew that three adults lived in the mulhaq (servants' quarters), I had absolutely no idea how many children lived there. The kids were always smiling and happy.

Today, the children did not look at all happy. I walked outside the gates, took one look at the Gulf Street and, sure enough, a formation of tanks was rumbling by. I noticed Iraqi soldiers on foot all armed with Kalashnikov AK47 automatic rifles. I quickly hopped back into our compound.

'What are you doing, Samir?' I asked.

It seemed a stupid question as he clasped a hose pipe in his hand and was pointing it at some flowers. A more pertinent question might have been: why are you watering the plants when a load of your countrymen are invading? Samir's English was not particularly good, but we always seemed to understand each other well enough. All the residents paid him to wash their cars and do various odd jobs and that was his living. Reward for his job as watchman, handyman and gardener was his very basic accommodation.

Poor old Samir was understandably not himself at all. I felt he must be just going through the motions, clinging to his routine. Over the coming weeks I did see him a few times and we talked a little. He told me that his fellow countrymen all believed they would be welcomed by the Kuwaiti people with open arms. They saw themselves as liberating their Kuwaiti brothers from the corrupt regime of the Al Sabah's (Kuwaiti royal family). They thought they would arrive as heroes and were shocked at their reception. The Kuwaitis hated them and behaved the way most people do when faced with an invading force that comes to ransack and occupy.

Martin, a colleague from the dealing room, arrived a short while later – obviously not via the Gulf Street. He was just in time for the fireworks. My apartment block was the last in a line facing the street. Next to my block was the Crown Prince's Palace surrounded by a large patch of desert. This open space surrounding the palace was to allow tower guards to spot any attack but in reality, it was used by all the local kids to play football.

I opened the gates to the compound and Martin drove in. Once inside my flat, he told me about his wake up experience. He heard a horrendous noise and his building was shaking. He lived on an upper floor and, not sure what was happening, went onto his balcony to investigate. It was then that he realised an invasion was underway. A shell smashed its way through the corner of his apartment block and he could see into his neighbour's living room. He heard small arms fire and ducked back into his flat. He knew that I lived in a ground floor apartment so called me and, after packing an overnight bag, made his way to join me.

'What was the drive over here like?' I asked.

'There are troops and military vehicles all over the place and they're starting to set up road blocks.'

We decided to go onto the roof of the three-storey building to see what was going on but at that moment all hell broke loose. The Iraqis were shelling the Crown Prince's Palace which, we later found out, was unoccupied. The whole of our building really started to shake and the noise was deafening. However, I did just about manage to hear Martin shouting, 'We should get close to a supporting wall, mate!'

'Right!' I screamed back at him. 'Which wall is a supporting one then?'

'I don't know. I thought that you might.'

'For fuck's sake Martin, why would I have any more idea than you? Do I look like a bloody builder?'

We both started to laugh, the shock and stress we felt suddenly finding a release.

Once the shelling stopped, we went to the roof to have a look around. We saw the Gulf Street full of tanks laboriously making their way south away from Kuwait city centre. There were troops scurrying about and huge plumes of smoke coming from the palace which was showing signs of the assault. The scene was like watching a news report from a war zone except that we were watching it live and could smell the action as well. I felt another adrenalin rush and a sense of terror and wondered if Martin was feeling the same. I turned to him, 'Christ, chief. I've seen enough. I'm going back inside.'

The rest of the day was spent on the phone. I first called the British Embassy and there was no reply. I called several times during the day and eventually, by the early evening, they had taken the time and trouble to leave an answer phone message. Basically, they advised us to stay indoors and off the streets. Wonderful! Marvellous! I'll just do that then.

For the first day or two we were able to make international calls although that stopped abruptly. Before international lines went down, I managed to get through to my father and brother. I also tried to get Mandy but she was out at the time. The national lines continued and the phone proved to be essential

Martin and Jim approximately ten days into the invasion.

keeping us in touch with everyone we knew without having to leave the apartment.

I pondered back to an earlier time when Mandy and I were enjoying a meal with friends. A good friend of my wife worked at the Embassy. Later she completed her placement and left the country. In the meantime she was getting heated and we let her rant, 'There are contingency plans in place for any given situation, including an invasion. If ever the situation arises where British subjects are in danger, RAF planes will arrive to evacuate every Brit who is on their register.'

The row took place when she discovered that, not only was I not registered at the Embassy, a heinous crime in itself, but the fact that I had not registered my wife or daughter was quite clearly a sin right up there in the top ten. Partially to keep my wife and her friend happy, but also because I thought it was a good thing to do, I registered us all.

The only way to describe those first few days after the invasion was 'headless chicken scenario'. We were clueless as to what to do and still somewhat in a state of shock. Through phone calls to friends and visits to neighbours in the block of flats, we were soon aware of all the rumour and gossip, of which there was plenty. The Royal Family had left by helicopter! The Embassy knew about the invasion many, many hours before the rest of us! I supposed they were going through the register and making calls, clearly not up to the Ps yet!

This corroborated murmurings I had heard regarding sightings of Embassy 4x4s at the Sultan Centre in the middle of the night before the invasion, causing mayhem with a jam of shopping trolleys, full to the brim. Apparently, their pool was emptied and refilled with water without the chlorine or chemicals. I believed them to be 'digging in' and already ruled out going to the Embassy as I was sure they would fob me off and send me home – that is if I actually managed to see anyone!

The following day, a friend of Martin's who hailed from the Lebanon, came round to check that he was ok and if he needed anything. He had been living in Beirut on two different occasions when fighting exploded. He laughed at us and shook his head.

'Have you guys done anything at all?'

Walking into the bathroom, he started to run the bath. I looked at Martin. 'Seems like a nice fellow, bit of an odd time for a bath, though.'

We both chortled. Michael came back into the lounge, 'Have you both managed to get to an ATM yet?'

We looked a bit crestfallen.

'No point trying now, the Iraqis are scavenging and they will be all over them. They'll mostly be empty anyway,' he said.

Michael took a quick look at the meagre supplies in the kitchen.

'Never mind. Let's have a drink.'

He pulled a bottle of Johnnie Walker Red Label out of his bag and we sat at my bar. What a thoroughly decent fellow, I thought. We were in our cups and all trying to put a bit of bravado on.

'Don't worry chaps, the British Embassy will be organising RAF planes to pick up everyone on their register as we speak. Mandy and Charlotte are back in the UK so you guys can have their seats. Yup, that sounds like a plan. Martin, you will be the Missus – ' I was interrupted.

'Jim, you're an idiot! Do you honestly think – ?'

'I know mate, I'm just trying to be funny.'

Late afternoon on 4 August, Ray was at the door. He owned and managed a real estate company and knew everybody. Hailing from Malta, this resourceful man spoke a few languages including Arabic. He married a Kuwaiti woman with whom he produced two lovely daughters. I felt a fierce blast of heat as I unlocked the door and let him in.

'Hey Jimbo! How is everything? Are you guys ok?'

After the usual pleasantries, he asked if Ali had been round. He had not.

'I called him around lunchtime and he said that he was coming to see you guys.'

We were halfway through a bottle of whisky discussing all the new developments of the occupation when Martin changed the subject, 'Why is Ali planning on coming round here?'

'Not too sure. He sounded a bit drunk, if I'm honest,' he sniggered.

Whilst we enjoyed a drink and good company, the sun passed over the yard arm. Curfew was now enforced and movement on the streets during the hours of darkness was strictly forbidden. We heard a car enter the compound and went to investigate. Ali fell out of the driver's seat and lay on the floor laughing. He was wearing pyjamas! His brother, whose name escapes me, was at least wearing a slightly dirty and dishevelled dishdasha (traditional male robe). He scuttled round the car, also crying with laughter and helped him to his feet. The two looked very shabby and I wondered how long they had been drinking.

As it was August, the heat was unbearable and so we quickly moved back into the comfort of air conditioning. With drinks flowing, our small party became quite jolly. The bottle was empty in no time and Ali threw his car keys to me, asking me to get a bottle from the boot of his car. I wobbled my way towards the door and, unbeknownst to me, he gathered my friends and followed me out.

Ali owned a big Yank tank. The boots in those things are enormous. When you remove everything from inside, they're even bigger. In place of the normal items found in a boot, spare wheel, etc, were bottles of scotch. These were taken out of their cardboard cases and laid in the boot. It was full to bursting! I couldn't even begin to estimate how many bottles they managed to squeeze in. With my jaw hanging open, I turned to the laughter as Ali geed up my friends. His humour was infectious and we went back into the flat in good spirits. We also took two bottles with us.

'Right, Ali. Let's hear all about it. What have you guys been up to?'

They looked like naughty schoolboys sniggering away as Ali regaled us regarding the 'heist'. We were all in hysterics as he told us how they broke into the customs house and filled their boot with as much whisky as they could carry.

Ali's brother asked if we wanted to buy any bottles and Ali lost his temper. He raged at his brother, said the bottles were a gift, thanked us for our hospitality, and they both left.

'What was that all about?' I asked no one in particular.

Ray answered, 'He was embarrassed that his brother raised the issue of money in front of his friends. Look, they're both really pissed. You know them. They will kiss and make up tomorrow.'

Now that a few days had passed, my initial feelings of panic and confusion were easing. We were still totally unprepared and, apart from packing an overnight bag, had made no plans whatsoever. I wondered how long before we lost the phone line, water and other utilities. I worried about food and what the future held for us. As time passed, I found it easier to control my emotions and took things a day at a time. I tried to only worry about those things I could affect. Fretting about events that were beyond my control was pointless.

I was in contact with a lot of people and always tried to put on a brave front. Inside I was awash with mixed emotions and knew that they felt the same. As a relatively young man of thirty-one, I had little cause to battle with thoughts of my own destiny but now, the thought of my life being prematurely ended, was ever present. The fact that I didn't mentally break down into a shivering, jibbering wreck, was as much due to my friends' support as my own willpower.

8

Run for the Border?

The Iraqi disagreements with Kuwait were not entirely spurious and I felt a little sympathy for them. Once threatened with aggression, the Kuwaitis wanted to make large concessions and were desperate to keep the peace, but Saddam was past listening and invaded. He was stopping me from leaving the country and so my sympathy turned to animosity and, until we were released, I considered him my enemy.

The TV babbled away in the background for most of the day. The news loop on CNN repeated itself ad infinitum but also brought us the breaking stories. As Westerners crossed the desert into Saudi Arabia, camcorder footage from the conflict in Kuwait city emerged. It was a bit weird watching our own situation and hearing about our plight on the telly.

There was worldwide condemnation for this 'act of naked aggression' and within three or four days all Iraqi and Kuwaiti assets were frozen. A total embargo on oil and goods was ratified by the UN and Saddam ordered to end the occupation. Both sides blustered but most of the sabre rattling came from Saddam. The Iraqis moved into their formations in the desert between

Kuwait city and Saudi Arabia. They settled into a routine. This gave an opportunity for groups of Westerners, either alone or with the help of Bedouins, to try to circumvent the troops and cross the border. Some were successful but others were taken by the enemy.

As well as television, the phone was a godsend. We were able to stay in contact with friends and keep each other abreast of developments. Information was passed on through a loose pyramid structure. I spoke with six or so people every few days who communicated with six others and so on. I was in regular contact with Steve who, with his wife, were the witnesses at my wedding. One conversation concerned the possibility of escape.

After hearing of Westerners fleeing to Saudi Arabia across the desert, there was a plan afoot involving a group from the banking community. Steve very kindly offered Martin and myself a place in their convoy. I pointed out that I owned a regular car designed for tarmac and didn't want to risk the sands. This was not a problem; he said that there were seats for us in their four-wheel drive vehicles. He thought the situation would only get worse with food becoming scarce and the Iraqis more hostile.

The troops were laying minefields now and so it was becoming more difficult to make for the border. Steve's view was now or never and they were leaving in two days. I let him know that I was touched by the offer and said that I would discuss it with Martin and call him back within the hour. I interrupted Martin's game of patience and ran through my recent phone conversation.

'What do you think?' I asked.

'I don't know; sounds a bit risky to me and we have no idea how far the Iraqis have got with their mine laying. I can understand wanting to go but I might hold on here for a bit and see how things pan out. Jim, you have to decide but as for me, I'm staying.'

Martin made up his mind so quickly I assumed he must have already been considering escape. My gut feeling was to stay put and take my chances in Kuwait; it is not an everyday occurrence to be in a war zone experiencing historic world events first hand. I made calls to my chain and gathered a mixed response regarding a run to the border. Lorraine, a friend married to a Kuwaiti pilot, decided she was staying. I had heard a rumour that the Iraqis were tapping the phones and I thought I heard suspicious noises on the line. I mentioned the rumour to Lorraine and she responded, 'People who listen in on other people's conversations are likely to hear things they don't want to hear.'

She endeared herself to me as I felt a national pride in her bulldog spirit. My final call was to Steve.

'Cheers, mate. I really appreciate the offer but we're going to hold out a bit longer. I wish you guys all the luck in the world.'

Three days later, while watching CNN, I saw one of their party being interviewed in Saudi Arabia and had mixed feelings. On the one hand I was glad and relieved that my friends were now safely out of Kuwait but on the other, a little bit jealous that I was not with them. Martin was also watching and, with raised eyebrows, took note when the interviewee said how smoothly everything had gone. We had a quick chat and settled that if the chance rose again, we would take it.

Another opportunity to run offered itself just two days later. Martin and I were in agreement that we would attempt the crossing on the following day, 13 August. During the evening of 12 August as we watched CNN, we learned the sad news that Douglas Croskery had been killed. He was close to the border when Iraqi troops sprayed the car he was travelling in with machine-gun fire. Our planned escape was cancelled and from this time on, fleeing across the desert became increasingly difficult with the Iraqis laying endless minefields.

Waleed, a colleague from work, came to visit and we sat enjoying a cup of coffee. He had just bought a tank for one thousand dinars – roughly two thousand pounds. The Iraqis in the tank were happy to take the money, change into civilian clothes and disappear into the populace. My friend saturated the tank with petrol and set fire to it. The Iraqis possessed one less tank and Waleed made a real blow on behalf of Kuwait. I admired his ingenuity and reflected on an age and place where a wallet was as important to the resistance as a bazooka.

The tension was building and the policy of the occupiers became more savage. I heard of the assassinations of some resistance members and how their bodies were dumped in front of their family homes. I urged my friend to take care. Others popped in that afternoon and there were half-a-dozen or so nationalities. Although many things were discussed, high on the agenda was Saddam's ultimatum that Westerners surrender themselves to named hotels or suffer 'unspecified difficulties'. The announcement brought another adrenalin rush.

The Iraqis were placing certain nationalities on strategic military sites to act as a human shield – a deterrent to US bombing. Amongst the Europeans it was Brits, Germans and French who were on the capture list. I was the only one sitting there who qualified for the human shield. With false bravado I told the others that I was not going to give myself up to anyone. An Irishman I didn't know arrived with a friend of mine and maintained that he had contacts in the Irish Embassy. He offered to get me an Irish passport – 'no bother at all.' Ha! I thought, I won't hold my breath.

When I went into the kitchen to get some ice, Waleed followed me in. More than a colleague, he was a trusted friend. I could see by his body language that he wanted to speak to me in private. Following the chaos that was the first few days of invasion, he got involved with the resistance movement. One of their first acts of rebellion was to gather food from the supermarkets, co-ops, and wholesale centres and hide it. My friend was heavily involved with that and later, in organising the food distribution. The Iraq troops relied on scavenging and this was causing them problems. As things became more desperate, a box of water could be traded for a Kalashnikov.

'Jim, the resistance are bringing in Kate Adie.'

'Good grief! Is she coming across the desert from Riyadh?' I asked.

'Yes. A senior Iraqi officer has been paid a lot of money to let her through their front lines and later, back through and across the border.'

'But what for? What does she hope to achieve?'

'The eyes of the world are on Kuwait right now.' He didn't need to expand upon the point.

Waleed looked me in the eye and said, 'Do you want to get out of Kuwait?'

I smiled, 'Of course. Do you think I'm some sort of simpleton?'

'I think I can get you into the car that is taking Kate Adie back to Riyadh.'

I felt a warm flush of excitement.

'What about Martin? Is there a space for him?'

'I'm afraid not, Jim. There's only one spare space.'

I thought back to moments when we were deep in our cups and swearing oaths of brotherhood. We promised to come through this adversity together. Considering our recent experiences, I knew that leaving Martin behind wasn't an option.

'Waleed, thank you so much. I really appreciate such a generous offer but it can't be done. I think Martin and I will take our chances together. Hang on a second! What about we leave Kate Adie here and Martin and I go out in the car?'

He belly laughed, thinking it was extremely funny, 'That's a good one, Jim. OK, I'm off. I'll be in touch soon.'

He wandered through the lounge, said his goodbyes and left.

For most the invasion was a frightening time and some coped better than others. Characters normally cool, calm and collected surprised me by behaving like headless chickens. In contrast, others I might have imagined to be hopeless and needy were conspicuous by their strength of will and ability to endure any given situation.

Then in a category all by himself was Bushby, a heavy drinker at the best of times, and now out of control. We were all drinking too much because of the long hours doing nothing, together with the constant, underlying, nagging fear, exacerbated on occasion to borderline terror. The sounds of conflict were ever present as the resistance and Iraqis fought on the streets. The alcohol dulled the senses, helped with sleep and filled the endless hours of sitting and worrying.

My Canadian friend had been running around Kuwait city like a thrill-seeker drinking heavily with all and sundry, enjoying what he called 'invasion parties'. The majority stayed indoors and only ventured out for food or emergencies and never after the hours of darkness when a strict curfew was enforced. Our friend would drive halfway across the city on a rumour that an Iraqi taxi driver was selling cases of Heineken.

Mid-afternoon, he arrived in his Saab 900 turbo. He had clearly been drinking for some time. His normally resplendent walrus moustache was half its normal size with the right side removed. He brought booze with him and Martin and I joined in. Sunset had been and gone an hour ago, so I assumed that he was staying the night. He asked to use the phone and re-joined us a few minutes later.

'There's a party in Jabriya, some Kuwaitis, some Europeans, all sorts really, are going. What do you think?'

Martin looked at me and rolled his eyes. We shared similar views on Bushby's unnecessary risk-taking.

'If you want to run around playing the idiot, then go right ahead. However you are very pissed and there is a curfew. So no! I won't be going to any party,' said Martin.

I smiled and chipped in, 'No! Before you ask.'

'Fair enough', and off he went.

In the middle of the night I answered the phone. It was my thrill-seeking chum in a state asking for help. He told me that he was involved in an accident and needed to go to the hospital. I managed to establish that he was at home and not in danger of imminent death! I told him that we would come to him in the morning. Once the sun was up, we headed to his place in Martin's car and found a very timorous individual. He had continued drinking and passed out on his floor. The blood from his head wound had fused to the carpet and he was in a lot of pain. On the way to the hospital, from his befuddled memory, we manged to piece together some of the events of the previous evening. He was involved in some sort of accident and crashed his car in a collision with a checkpoint. He had no idea why the Iraqis hadn't grabbed him but he remembered some Kuwaitis taking him home. The doctor reported that he needed stitches but wanted a cash payment. Martin handed over some Kuwait dinars and the doctor stitched him up. We all returned to my apartment where a very subdued Bushby stayed for a day or two, feeling sorry for himself, much to our amusement.

Over the coming days tensions rose. The Iraqis were sweeping south from the Kuwait International hotel which they were using as a headquarters. They were searching apartments and villas looking for Westerners to take hostage, and looting as they went. The military activity surrounding us increased and both Martin and I felt vulnerable. I called Ray and left a message at his home. Some hours later he came round and, before I could say anything, he said that he didn't think it was safe to remain in my flat.

Ray possessed the keys to an apartment in the Al-Tameer complex which belonged to a Saudi gentleman who was out of the country. The good news was that the fridge and freezer were stocked, as was the bar. The bad news was that it was roughly fifty yards from the Kuwait International, a nest full of the enemy. After some discussion we tried to put a positive slant on things and all agreed that they would have cleared the area immediately adjacent to the hotel. We were between a rock and a hard place and decided to make the move. The following day, at first light, we planned to follow Ray in Martin's car to our new hideout.

The Al-Tameer complex, our second hiding spot.

9
Move to a New Hideout

While waiting for Ray at dawn, a depressing thought crossed my mind that I might not see my belongings again. This had been my life and I was leaving it all behind. I hadn't received my end of term settlement and so it seemed that the last three years of my life were for nothing. In fact, if I was offered just the clothes that I stood up in, but back in the UK, I would have accepted in a second.

When he arrived we spent a short time listening to a very ad hoc sort of plan. I was the only one among us on the list of nationalities destined for the human shield but that didn't mean that Martin and Ray were free from risk themselves. The invading Republican Guard were well-trained professional soldiers but they were replaced by the occupying force who were decidedly shabby to say the least. They shouldn't be in charge of a car, let alone a gun and accidents were bound to happen. We planned to avoid the Gulf Street and other main thoroughfares and make our way through the back streets. We wouldn't stop unless forced to and, if we got separated, we would reunite back at my flat.

The journey was completely uneventful. We stuck to the minor roads and didn't encounter anyone at all. I was shocked by how quickly the city had deteriorated, scarred by the acts of war. The city that once thronged with life, stood empty, a fragment of its former self. Charred buildings, pock-marked with bullet holes, were left in ruins. Scattered piles of concrete and rubble were commonplace. Broken store fronts were laid waste, evidence of wholesale looting. We made it to the underground carpark and breathed a sigh of relief. On entering the lift Ray told us that there were two Filipino women living in the apartment and I thought that he was pulling my leg until he knocked on the door and it was answered by Virgie.

We all sat in the lounge and Ray made the introductions. Gloria had known Ray for some time. She moved in with her friend Virgie once the invasion was underway. Virgie and Gloria went to prepare breakfast and Ray told us that he thought things would work out. They had been scared on their own, particularly at night when skirmishes between the Iraqis and the resistance often erupted. Virgie returned with food and coffee. Martin and I dug in.

The two women wandered off on some pretext and the three of us flopped on the sofas in the lounge of the luxurious apartment. Needless to say we were profuse in our gratitude to Ray which he made light of. While on route near the main souk, he saw a man hanging from a crane. There had been word of hangings, rape and other atrocities but now we were hearing a first-hand account. The atmosphere darkened for a moment.

'Where did the girls go?' asked Martin, lightening the mood.

'God only knows! They worry me those two,' replied Ray.

We watched CNN and I was amazed at the speed of the

military build-up. Warships were in the Gulf, and US troops were deploying to Saudi Arabia. The scale of the operation was impressive. Saddam was calling for Jihad, a holy war against the West. He wanted the Arab nations to unify behind the Palestinian cause. As two-thirds of the members of The Arab League of Nations had already condemned his actions, his chances were slim at best. There was some mention of the plight of stranded Westerners in Kuwait which piqued our interest and elicited a partisan cheer.

We reached the time of day when the sun was scorching and a nap seemed like a good idea. Virgie and Gloria returned with bags filled with cans of soft drinks and Ray said his goodbyes. The apartment was well-appointed for bedrooms and I was shown to one where I tried, unsuccessfully, to sleep. Under normal circumstances, my sleep pattern was fairly regular but since the invasion, it was at sixes and sevens – sometimes I was unable to sleep even when feeling exhausted. Martin's snoring indicated that he didn't suffer the same problem!

I was not managing myself very well when experiencing these intense rushes of adrenalin and their subsequent comedown. When dealing, I sometimes experienced similar feelings but these were different. These were triggered by fear rather than excitement. The rush can be addictive and it is understandable why people engage in extreme sports and other forms of thrill-seeking. I dressed and made my way very circumspectly onto the balcony. From this vantage point there was a good view of the surroundings. The city was starting to resemble Beirut. As I checked out the locale, two Iraqi soldiers walked into view so I quickly ducked back inside.

We all became firm friends, with Martin and Virgie forming

a special relationship. Virgie and Gloria were always good humoured and their resourcefulness in providing tasty meals every day was very much appreciated. We played card games and the TV was ever present, regurgitating the pompous diatribes of strutting politicians on both sides of the conflict.

(Writing this thirty years later, I can confirm that we are still good friends. Gloria and Ray live together in Malta, and Martin and Virgie in Holland. We formed bonds that could only have developed under such extreme circumstances. These guys are family to me.)

We settled into our new accommodation and, while hearing of more atrocities, we were hiding in relative comfort. The news was quiet and I started to have feelings of despair – the problem being that we had very little to do except reflect on our dire situation. I wanted to scream or bash my head against a wall with the increasing frustration. Things did pick up over the coming days. Jordan closed its border with Iraq and then, on 18 August, two US warships fired warning shots across the bows of two Iraqi oil tankers. Saddam called the embargo and its enforcement an act of war. Out of the blue, on the following day, Saddam offered to let us go!

We were extremely excited because we believed that this might lead to some positive dialogue. Saddam's offer was conditional on the lifting of the worldwide trade embargo and the disbanding of the coalition troops in Saudi Arabia. This sounded good to me but, of course, he was not prepared to leave Kuwait so it would all come to nought.

The capture of Western civilians and placing them on strategic military sites as human shields received worldwide condemnation. Using us as bargaining chips just increased the general feelings of disgust. Our emotions were stretched to the limit and I hoped that this offer might at least open lines of communication. I was smashed down to earth a few days later when I listened to a speech by Mrs Thatcher in her D-Day mood. Her speech was full of rhetoric; she would never be blackmailed or bargain on behalf of the hostages.

She took a hard stance as was expected of the Iron Lady and even criticised the Red Cross for not doing more. Our prime minister, true to form, would not compromise and, while I admired the strong leadership, I wished that it didn't involve me. Like buses, the news items came along in batches of twos or threes and, sure enough, Saddam decided to stir the pot. He offered to leave Kuwait if Israel left the occupied territories in Palestine. You had to laugh to stop yourself from crying. I asked if anybody wanted a drink.

'It's a little early, chief!'

'Don't give a shit! I feel like getting hammered,' I let them all know.

The girls were not up for it and disappeared off into another room. We started to drink heavily and were thoroughly enjoying ourselves. Virgie and Gloria popped into the lounge from time to time to laugh at our drunken antics. That evening we heard the sounds of a fire fight coming closer. The strict curfew meant that anyone on the streets after dark was fair game. The resistance were attacking Iraqi troops in and around our complex of tower blocks.

Still inebriated, we thought it was a good idea to go onto the balcony to watch the 'fireworks'. With the lights off, we crept onto the balcony and sat watching the show – completely surreal and bizarre to say the least! We saw the skirmish unfold as though we were in our directors' chairs on a film set. It certainly knocked spots off watching war films on the telly. We started to add a running commentary pointing out individuals to each other and commenting on the state of play. Someone spotted us and raised his Kalashnikov in our general direction letting off a few rounds. We were back inside in a nanosecond and that was the end of that little game!

The following day, nursing a hangover, I listened to a statement from the Iraqi regime. They increased the tension still further by threatening the Kuwaitis. Any Kuwaiti caught harbouring or giving aid to Westerners may well be put to death.

I opened the door to Waleed and gave him a stern look, 'I told you on the phone not to come round here.'

My friend bridled at that, 'That is not the way to invite me into your home,' he said.

'You're a great friend and I admire your bravery, I really do. Waleed please! Tell me why on earth you are here.'

'I've come to visit you. What is your problem?'

I was starting to get annoyed. He was being obtuse. He clearly just thought of an idea and added, 'I came to see how you are doing for food.'

'Follow me,' I said and we went into the kitchen.

I opened the freezer and the fridge to reveal that they were both adequately stocked. I lowered my tone and said, 'You can see we are alright for food. We're ok! If and when I need something, you will be the first guy I call. Don't tell me you haven't heard the latest directive from Saddam. You know he will do it. You will be killed if you are caught helping us.'

I hoped that I had got my point across. My argument was

succinct enough but, then again, apparently not.

'If you think I care anything about that snake, that backstabbing shit of the worst kind, a usurper – '

I tried to cut him off but he spoke over the top of me, 'This is my country. You are my friend. You are invited to be here. That dog from Baghdad is not invited. He is not on our guest list. Fuck him! He will not tell me what to do in my own country.'

I took a deep breath and raised my voice, 'Look! Calm down for goodness sake. You know you don't need to prove anything. Your kindness since the invasion will stay with me forever. Listen, mate, this isn't about you. I'm the one who couldn't live with myself if I caused your wife to become a widow and your children fatherless. Your wife is pregnant right now! She must be going crazy with worry. Look to your family my friend and I promise, hand on heart, I will call you if there is anything I need.'

He nodded and I knew that he might well continue with his risk-taking but I desperately hoped that he might be a little more circumspect going forward.

'Well, you're here now! Do you want something – tea or coffee maybe?' I asked him.

Iraq ordered Embassies in Kuwait to relocate to Baghdad and surrounded the ones that were not complying with troops. I thought the British Embassy might as well go because they were doing very little for the Brits trapped in Kuwait as far as I could see. The pressure was increased even further when Ali Hassan al-Majid was appointed Governor as he was supposed to be a hardliner. On the very day of his appointment, a pregnant British woman was arrested at a road block when returning from an antenatal class.

August ended and nearly a month had passed. I was extremely angry with the British government. We were an irritation only to be used for propaganda purposes. They used us mercilessly in the world press as an example of how evil the Butcher of Baghdad was – killing his own people with chemical weapons. The British Embassy and Foreign Office were both conspicuous by their absence. They not only refused to send these so-called planes to airlift us to safety but gave very little in the way of advice. Their advice was to stay indoors and not attempt any escape. With hindsight, a flight to the border within two or three days of the invasion might have been the best option.

Martin wearing a gas mask provided by the
Dutch Embassy.

Jim following British Embassy guidelines.

On 6 September we finally heard from the government via a statement from the Foreign Office. They seemed keen that Brits should not resist arrest – and thank goodness they finally got around to that because later that night we were captured. How on earth I could have managed to cope with this terrible ordeal without their pearls of wisdom one can only imagine.

10

Captured and Blindfolded

Eleven-thirty pm, twenty republican guards, armed to the teeth, knocked down the door to our refuge. Martin looked at me, 'Well that's a little overdone, don't you think?'

As we only possessed a fly swat and a pack of well-worn playing cards, I had to agree with him. Earlier we heard them in the apartment block and knew that they were scavenging. We discussed the idea of hiding but dismissed it as a non-starter. Much later, I wondered if I was perhaps a little relieved; that overwhelming fear of capture disappeared. We all heard rumours of ill treatment experienced by some Westerners after the invasion. A German woman was raped at gunpoint while her husband was tied up and made to view the horrendous spectacle. We heard many other tales of atrocities. Propaganda often starts at street level, to encourage resistance and a building of hatred for the invader.

Martin and I sat in the lounge with Virgie and Gloria. The soldiers just stood watching us. After a few minutes which seemed like a lifetime, Martin made eye contact with me and we shrugged our shoulders. An officer came into the lounge. He was quite young and dressed in jodhpurs and a flying jacket – I kid you not! He sported a peaked cap and highly-polished riding boots. I was worried that, with the adrenalin coursing through my veins, I might burst out laughing as visions of *Russ Abbott's Madhouse* came to mind. This really must be a nightmare. Perhaps I'll wake up soon! The young Iraqi officer approached and seemed a bit put out when he left the marbled tiled area and walked onto the shag pile carpet because his boots were no longer making the Nazi jackboot sound. In perfect English, he asked our nationalities and to hand over passports. He told us to pack a bag. Then he shouted in Arabic and soldiers started to ransack the apartment, stealing anything that wasn't nailed down. I quickly pushed my way into the bedroom and picked up my holdall before it too disappeared into their thieving hands. I went swiftly back in the lounge where the girls had not moved. Virgie said, 'It's ok, Jim, we are staying.'

I said to the officer, 'I hope these ladies are going to be safe. Can you ensure their safety?'

He was really angry and started to rant, 'What kind of people do you think we are? We are not animals!'

I tried to show as much contrition as possible and apologised profusely. I said that I had heard stories but could tell that he was a gentleman of honour or some such bullshit. He calmed down and started to smile when Martin walked in and said, 'You'd better make sure that none of these monkeys touches the girls!'

My heart skipped a beat as I intervened, 'There's no need to worry, Martin. I've spoken with the officer. He is clearly a man of honour and has given his assurance that the girls will not be harmed.'

We said our goodbyes to Virgie and Gloria, grabbed our bags and were taken to a make-shift camp. The soldiers who broke into our apartment were Republican Guard and looked very professional. This lot milling around the camp were slovenly, wore mismatched uniforms and odd assortments of t-shirts and trainers. We were handed over to the camp commander and were offered tea. We were existing in a pressure cooker with constant fear of capture and I had never experienced anything like it. The adrenalin rush was over, leaving me feeling drained but curiously elated. I had been captured and yet I hadn't been buggered or shot. I took this as a positive and was feeling quite chipper, given the situation.

We were brought to the camp for some sort of processing and while drinking the sticky tea, I asked what was in store for us. The commander's English was not good but I understood that he was waiting for orders from above. We sat in the office for a few hours. The heat was oppressive and I was starting to nod off when soldiers entered. They collected a file of paperwork including our passports and marched us out to a four-wheel drive. Things took a downward turn and my feeling of wellbeing instantly disappeared when they blindfolded us at gunpoint and shoved us into the vehicle. My heart dropped into my stomach and fear tingled up my spine – if these fuckers were trying to scare me, they were doing a good job.

We drove around for hours making occasional stops. My fear escalated with the clamour of men getting into and out of the car, all shouting over each other in Arabic. I felt the vehicle leave the tarmac as we started to bump around and I guessed that we were being driven down a desert track. A short while later we stopped and the soldiers dragged us out and stood us side by side. This was not my day and I imagined it being my last. I experienced the bizarre feeling that my arms were stretching towards the ground, clearly made of elastic. My shoulders seemed incapable of fulfilling their supporting role. I heard Martin say, 'Put me back in the car or shoot me in the head because I've had enough of this.'

Respect for my Dutch pal rose to a new level. His reaction was perhaps not what they were expecting. We were quickly bundled back into the car, and it sped off. After a short time we were told to take off the blindfolds and we found ourselves at the Meridien Hotel where our nightmare experience ended – albeit for a brief time. Hindsight is a wonderful thing and later I realised that they were just playing with us. At the time, I was of a different frame of mind and wracked with fear.

Now that I was no longer blindfolded, I could see that the man next to me, who was trying to rearrange my ribcage with his AK47, was in plain clothes. He had cold, dark eyes and I decided he was a complete bastard. This self-important dickhead was spouting all sorts of rhetoric. He was possibly a Ba'ath party zealot. He told me exactly what he thought of 'Me-sees Tatcher'. Clearly it was my job to tell everyone back in 'Blighty' how our prime minister was evil. I couldn't keep my mouth shut and suggested he should fly me to the UK and I would go and see her personally. The armed Iraqi was not amused so I firmly clamped my mouth shut before I got myself into serious trouble.

Once out of the car, Martin was given his passport and told to go home. The Dutch were not on the capture list for foreign hostages and at that moment I really wished I was Dutch. I asked if I could have my passport back and was told 'Me-sees Tatcher'.

My pal and I hugged each other which I found a little strange. He wasn't the most touchy-feely sort of chap under normal circumstances. However, these were not normal circumstances. His kindness and friendship touched me deeply and it was an emotionally charged moment.

'Be strong, Jimbo. Take care and try not to worry. I will do my best to contact your embassy and let them know what has happened.'

I smiled, thanked him, uttered a few inane comments and entered the Meridien Hotel with my plain-clothes escort.

At the reception desk I was asked to check in. Just another surreal moment! I was abducted at gunpoint, blindfolded and now I was being asked to bloody well check in like any regular guest. It was now five-thirty am, six hours since my capture and the plain-clothes Iraqi told me to be ready for eight-thirty am when a bus would take us to Baghdad. He said that I was to be a 'guest' of Saddam Hussein and left the hotel. There were Iraqi soldiers all over the place with what appeared to be guards at the doors watching who came and went.

I took the lift for my room and noticed two soldiers sitting on chairs in the corridor. I ignored them, entered my room and smoked a cigarette. I tried to think rationally but my thoughts were all over the place. Maybe two hours sleep and a shower might help. I threw myself on the bed and drifted into a coma. I awoke with two Iraqis in plain clothes roughly shaking me awake. I pulled myself together and, once I was dressed, they took me into an office. I was fully awake by now, with a fresh wave of adrenalin once again flooding through my body. They asked me where my British friends were living and I replied that I was fairly new to the country and didn't really know many people. I told them that the few people that I did know had left for the summer. They accepted this and told me that I could go. Back in the room, I lay down again but couldn't get back to sleep. My body was crying out for complete rest but my brain wouldn't switch off. My sleeping patterns had gone all to hell since the invasion and I had been awake for the last thirty hours.

Sleep deprived as I was, there was no chance I was going to nod off, so I took a bath and suddenly remembered, all in a panic, about the letter. A friend told me he was getting out through Jordan on a Jordanian passport he acquired and offered to take any letters out for me. I wrote a letter to my wife but hadn't managed to contact my friend since writing it and it was at the bottom of my bag. I am afraid I was a bit scathing about Iraqis in general and President Saddam Hussein in particular. I must have been a trifle unbalanced, but after burning the letter and flushing the ashes down the toilet, I felt a lot calmer.

At about eight am I went down to the lobby in search of a coffee. The coffee shop manager took my room number and showed me to the breakfast buffet. The fare was meagre, to say the least, with watermelon, stale bread, jam and coffee on offer. There were a lot of soldiers all jabbering away and, after an initial glance, they mostly ignored me. I spotted one guy in western clothes and took a black coffee and joined him at his table.

'Good morning,' he said. 'My name is Dominic. When were you taken?'

'I'm Jim Payne and I was taken last night.'

'They are bastards! Eat something, mon ami.'

I told my new ally that I didn't think I could eat; that I was happy with a coffee and a Marlboro.

'Eat something, my friend. You will thank me later.'

I was drained and couldn't be bothered arguing so I ate a little.

'Are you going to Baghdad today?' I asked.

'No, it is not possible. They will not send a bus for just three people,' he replied.

'Three?'

'Yes, there is a Pakistani being held here also.'

I had believed all Asians were free to come and go but Dominic explained. The gentleman in question was a civilian working for the Kuwait Air Force. He was denounced to the Iraqis by a Palestinian he knew whilst trying to withdraw money from his bank account. They handcuffed and blindfolded him, taking him off for interrogation. This occurred within days of the invasion and since then he had been held in a camp and given a pretty hard time of it. He was brought to The Meridien with just the clothes he stood up in to be transported to Baghdad alongside any Westerners they also managed to capture.

'Listen, mon ami, these savages are fucking bastards and I spit on them!'

With that he looked towards the nearest Iraqi soldiers and with great Gallic flair, hawked and spat a big glob of phlegm on the floor. The Iraqis bridled and half rose from their seats. Dominic just stared at them. Good god, I thought, why on earth did I sit down next to this tool? I did like his attitude though. The tension was building when a young woman wearing The Meridien uniform walked into the coffee shop.

'Telephone for Jim Payne. Paging Jim Payne.'

I stood up.

'I'm Jim Payne.'

I left Dominic and the Iraqi soldiers to their stand off and followed the young lady to the house phone. This situation was getting more bizarre by the minute!

'Hello?'

'Hi Jim. Are you ok?' asked Ray.

'Yeah. I'm ok. How did you find out I was here so fast?'

'I went round to see Gloria and pop in on you guys. She told me what happened.'

'How are the girls?' I asked.

'They are fine. The Iraqis cleared the place out and then just left.'

'Thank god. What about Martin?'

'He got back to the apartment a short while ago and is sleeping.' His tone of voice changed slightly and became conspiratorial. 'Jim, can you get to the kitchens? I can get a car to the alley at the back of the hotel.'

I loved this guy! Situations like this bring out the best and worst in people. Ray was clearly a real trooper.

'Thanks Ray. You are a star. I can't do it though, pal. There are soldiers everywhere. Every door is watched and to be honest with you I am a bit broken right now.'

'Ok, ok, don't worry. Things will work out. We will get through this. Look, I'd better go. Take care and I'll see you.'

I replaced the phone with a tear in my eye. I so appreciated his concern and kindness. I wanted another coffee and went for a refill. Dominic was still at the table but the soldiers had left.

'If we aren't going to Baghdad, I think I'll go and get some sleep.'

Once back in my room, I decided to leave Martin to his sleep and called my Canadian friend.

'Hello, Bushby. It's Jim.'

'It's a bit early, chief.'

'Listen. I've been captured!'

'You think you've got problems. I can't find soft drinks anywhere. I'm actually drinking milk with my ethanol!'

'You really are a shithead! Tell Martin that I'm on my way to Baghdad today. He might be able to get through to the British Embassy although I'm not sure why we should bother – they will do fuck all!'

'I'm really sorry, mate. I'll touch base with Martin today, I promise. Take care, Jim, and I'll see you later.'

I wondered why my friends were so confident in seeing me later. I wished for their confidence. It was now ten am. I got into bed and fell into a deep sleep.

11

A Bus Full of Hostages

At mid-day, I was woken by a loud banging. An Iraqi in plain clothes ordered me down to the lobby as a bus was on its way. Dominic was passing and popped his head through the door.

'Are you ready to go?' I asked

'I am but you're not,' he said, looking around.

'Strip your room, my friend – soap, toilet rolls, the bottled water, towels, take it all.'

Good grief, I mused. Not for the first time I wondered why I was saddled with this clown. I grabbed the aforementioned items and down to the lobby we went. Through the glass frontage I watched the Iraqi soldiers teaching themselves how to drive. I went outside, lit a cigarette and viewed the spectacle. With half-a-dozen stolen cars was a sight not dissimilar to banger racing. I think I was actually smiling when a bus arrived, already three-quarters full.

The bus had set off from the Hyatt Regency Hotel where Westerners were ordered to give themselves up and avoid the unpleasantries of being captured. A lot of men with families took up this offer because women and children were being flown out of the country. They knew they were going straight on to the human shield but accepted this fate in exchange for their families' safety. A few weeks earlier the majority of families with children had already surrendered. As food became scarcer and conditions more difficult, it was now couples who were giving themselves up.

Dominic approached and carried my bag with him.

'Don't I have to check out?'

He laughed and threw my bag at me. We boarded, said our hellos to everyone and took two seats towards the back of the bus. Apart from the three of us who had just joined, the mix of passengers was an assortment of roughly fifty percent Americans, forty percent British and ten percent others. There were about thirty of us in total. I remember there was a French woman with her poodle; not my favourite dog but this one was quiet and well behaved. The Yanks were chattering incessantly without saying very much although one American woman sitting near us was very calm and kind. A driver, two guards armed with hand guns and a car following with four soldiers, all carrying AK47s, made up our small convoy.

The trip was uneventful until we reached the Iraq border where there was a huge log-jam of cars waiting to cross. I watched an old Arab gentleman dressed in the local garb, shouting at a driver of a flat-bed truck. The truck was crammed to bursting with TVs, video recorders, white goods and other domestic appliances.

'Ali Baba!' he was shouting at the driver.

He wielded a piece of metal pipe about three feet long and was attempting to smash the goods on the truck. The driver got out and was wrestling with the old fellow. Two soldiers were watching the scene and laughing. They shouted to the old man who completely ignored them. They yelled at him some more, then approached and clubbed him a couple of times with the butts of their rifles. Dominic, a fluent Arab speaker, explained the old guy was calling them thieves, scum and other insults. He accused them of robbing their brothers.

The checkpoint was informed of our passage and we were speedily waved through the throng. Looking through the window, I saw a car hissing and spouting steam from the radiator. Next to the car was a large woman jumping up and down with apoplexy. I thought she was just mad at her car but some of the Americans started hopping around as well. I gathered they knew her and that she had missed the bus from The Hyatt. We stopped and the fat woman with a French accent puffed and panted her way onto the bus. My French buddy decided he should introduce himself to her; maybe he was keen to speak his own language. He quickly resumed his seat next to me. 'French huh! I suspect she is Lebanese that one.'

I was completely uninterested and just smiled. Once we crossed the border, the flies became more plentiful and obnoxious. I was sure that this was more to do with the sweltering heat rather than the nationality of these pests. I swatted one on the headrest in front of me with the palm of my hand.

'Fifteen-love,' muttered my Gallic chum. As I wiped the fly off my hand, Dominic swatted two in quick succession, 'Thirty-fifteen.'

As our fly tennis match continued, I noticed that the Frenchman was leaving all these dead bugs on his hand and thought it a bit strange. One of the guards wandered down the aisle smiling and trying to be friendly to everyone. Dominic offered his hand to the guard and deftly manged to wipe a multitude of dead flies onto his hand. The smile on the Iraqi's face disappeared and was replaced with a snarl.

'I hope you enjoy. You son of a bitch,' said Dominic.

My nerves were strung as tight as a snare drum and I was still a bit light-headed from lack of sleep. It was as though a release valve was opened and I collapsed with laughter for a good few minutes, thoroughly enjoying the antics of this French maverick. I felt a bond was being forged and we got to talking.

He left France aged eighteen. He was a paratrooper and went to fight in Algeria. Unable to settle in France after he left the army, he returned to North Africa. In the twenty or so years since, he spent all his time in Arab-speaking countries. He was currently living with his third wife, an Egyptian woman of Bedouin descent, in Cairo. He maintained that he was in Kuwait on business! We talked at length and found a lot of common ground. Amongst peals of laughter, I formed a friendship with this bear of a man.

Our first stop after the border crossing was a toilet break. At the side of the road, was a smattering of scrub providing a modicum of cover for our modesty. The men were allowed to go behind the scrub in pairs. I think their reasoning was security against us running away. Once again, they baffled me. The majority of people on the bus willingly gave themselves up! Where on earth were we going to run to anyway? The landscape was barren for as far as the eye could see. We were travelling through some of the most gruesome looking desert there was in the Middle East. The scene would have made a great backdrop for a 1960s sci-fi B-movie. The ladies declined to use the facilities.

Once underway, I turned towards Dominic, 'What a shit-hole! I've never seen anything like it.'

'This used to be some of the most fertile land in Iraq, palm trees heaving with dates, tomatoes, cucumbers, and not too long ago either,' he replied.

'So what happened?' I asked.

'Saddam was intent on a building programme. He decided that bricks were more important than dates.'

He pointed to a long, low structure that didn't exactly look permanent. Adjoining was a small shanty town, presumably for the workers. 'There, you see. That is a brick factory.'

He went on to explain how they raped the top soil for bricks and then relocated a few miles down the road. The factories had turned a vast area into a moon-scape.

A guard came down the bus with a jug of water every hour or so. He filled a cup and once quaffed, he refilled and passed to the next person. We were certainly not going to dehydrate before reaching Baghdad. Early evening, we received a stale cheese sandwich, one per person. I remembered Dominic berating me to eat and he proved right – I was famished. I ate the grotty sandwich with relish.

'What do you think is going to happen?' I asked

'You must learn patience, my friend. Take each day as it comes. You must learn the meaning of Maktoob.'

'Right-o! What does Maktoob mean?'

'The Arabs believe that everything you do is already predetermined. Allah has a big ledger on which is recorded your birth, what happens in your life and your death. That is all. You have no influence, so just sit back and let it happen.'

'How bloody stupid!' I chipped in.

'This is why they are happy to fight and die for Jihad. They know that they will go straight to Allah for everlasting heaven.'

'That is just so stupid – or perhaps convenient. If, for example, someone is caught stealing then technically, it is not his fault as it is written in the ledger.'

'True, that is true! It may also be written that you get your hand chopped off.'

I was smiling as I tried to get my head around this new concept.

'You have no control over your own destiny for the time being, my friend,' he added.

We pulled off the road and the driver immediately lit a cigarette. A look of pleasurable relief washed over his face. A discussion between the driver and Iraqi soldiers went on for a few minutes. Dominic was struggling with the regional dialect but managed to grasp that we were missing our escort. Eventually the driver executed a U-turn and we retraced our steps. A short while later, we saw our fellow travellers at the side of the road. Their car was jacked up and a wheel with a flat tyre was leaning against it. The Iraqi soldiers were all shouting at the same time and the situation appeared heated.

'This should be interesting,' said Dominic, smiling.

Clearly the tyre was punctured but the accompanying spare wheel did not fit the car. Our 'boys' were frazzled and completely stumped. Dominic laughed and our bus guards gave him a dirty look.

'You see, Jim, this is not part of the "routine". They have adopted the concept as a science and it suits their make-up very well. You see they will not abandon the car and join the bus because of routine. They cannot drive the car because the spare wheel does not fit. As if this 'catch-22' is not bad enough, they have a timetable to keep and may be in some trouble if late.'

He was cheerful and seemed very amused at their conundrum. 'Jim, just look at these stupid bastards!'

'Couldn't organise a piss up in a brewery!' was my response.

It was perfect timing for a joke making a comparison with our Gallic chums. I wasn't sure of the extent of his sense of humour yet and he was a bloody big bloke so I kept my thoughts to myself.

Fair play to the soldiers. They did manage to sort out their problem. A car of the same make and model was flagged to a stop. The soldiers ordered the Filipino occupants out of the car at gun point. After rejecting their spare as substandard, they were made to take a wheel off their own car. The guards gave the poor sods the punctured wheel in exchange and, after some manoeuvring, we were underway once again.

Our bus left the main road and, after travelling down a dirt track, we came across a dilapidated building with just two walls left standing. All eight women left the bus and went behind the walled shelter together. For the first and only time during our trip, the poodle whined a little but didn't actually bark. The dog strained at its leash being held by a male companion but was soothed and placid once again when reunited with its owner. Two of the guards from the car following joined our bus and I wondered why. I quickly put it out of my mind, marking it down to the beginnings of paranoia. Our journey was taking an age, partly because of the described stops and starts but also because of the endless army check points where we slowed down to a crawl. The rest of the journey was uneventful and I even managed a brief sleep.

I awoke to find Dominic asleep. A few rows in front sat Colin with whom I had already passed a few words. He was awake and I settled in next to him. 'Were you captured or did you hand yourself in?' I asked.

Colin explained that he was in hiding with his colleague Patrick somewhere near the Hyatt Regency. A head popped up from the row in front and gave me a smile and a nod. Following an invitation to be 'guests', at gunpoint, they were taken straight to the hotel for processing. He commented that they were treated with courtesy. I told them about my capture and they were shocked.

'No, nothing like that happened to us,' they both said.

We passed an anti-aircraft barrage a short distance from the road and I could see Colin making a mental note. I gave him the raised eyebrows.

'I did my National Service close to the border back in the day. Mind you, it was a British protectorate back then. I'm interested in all things militaria and have noticed their troop deployments. For example, did you notice that tank formation near the Mutla ridge is made up of busted tanks? You could see Iraqi soldiers getting the low loaders ready to move them a few miles down the road. They will be moved under cover of darkness where they will be set in a different formation facing a different direction.'

'What's the point of that?' I enquired.

'Well, when aerial reconnaissance is taken at different times, it will look like a moving tank formation instead of a moving scrapyard.'

It made sense and I listened to him as he enthused on a subject close to his heart.

Eighteen hours after leaving Kuwait city, we finally arrived at our destination, the Al-Mansour Melia hotel, in Baghdad. The driver was behind the wheel the whole time and drove very well. Here was a man to be commended on a job well done. Everyone was knackered, ready for a quick sandwich and bed. We were all kept waiting in the lobby, however, as various members of the Iraqi administration ran around like headless chickens.

12
Al-Mansour Melia Hotel Part 1

Before we left Kuwait, and unbeknownst to me, Dominic was in contact with the French Embassy. The arrangement made was that they would call him as soon as we arrived in Baghdad. Sure enough, and goodness knows how they knew that we had arrived, a page told him that he was wanted on the phone.

The Iraqis eventually managed to sort themselves out and started a roll call. When your name was read out you collected your bag and went to the lift area. An Iraqi official became very animated when Dominic didn't respond to his name. When it was pointed out that the subject of his frustration was on the phone, he lost all remaining composure. His jaw dropped and for a moment he stared at the Frenchman in disbelief. With steam coming out of his ears, he raced across the foyer and shouted various Arab obscenities at his French guest. My friend with absolute aplomb turned to the Iraqi officer, 'Do you mind? I'm trying to hold a phone conversation.'

He quickly finished and with the officer shaking his head, Dominic collected his bag and joined us by the lift. We were ordered out on the eighth floor where we milled around while the Iraqis went into their headless chicken routine once again. Eventually, some keys were brought and we were allocated rooms. We chose to share with each other, which seemed to cause a major problem as we were of different nationalities. We both strode into the room and dropped our bags on the beds, ending the dilemma.

A meal was arranged and scheduled for about twenty minutes time. I lay on my bed and smoked a cigarette. I knew I should write a letter but I felt far too tired. I decided that after dinner was soon enough. We left our room and walked down the corridor where four armed guards were deployed. We thought this a little ridiculous! What exactly were they doing? We joined the other 'happy campers' in the dining room. Dominic made a beeline for the French table while I decided that a bit of mingling was in order. I sat down at a table of men who looked like the bottom had fallen out of their world. They were all silent.

'Good evening, everybody,' I said with a smile.

'Is this a four or five star establishment?' I asked, while flicking a dead fly off the soiled tablecloth.

Very little response to my repartee was forthcoming but a middle-aged Scotsman caught my eye and grinned. A conversation of sorts broke out but it was all pretty miserable. I tried to gather as much information as I could but they all seemed as much in the dark as me. A hotel employee came into the room and announced that the meal would be ready in one hour.

An American exploded, completely losing the plot. Bordering on apoplexy, his assault was only verbal and had no effect whatsoever. The tension in the room was palpable. I asked the employee if we could have coffee straight away. There was a murmur of approval from the room and, with a look of relief on his face, the employee nodded and scuttled off.

The meal was ready. At the back of the large hall was a stage. Two full-length curtains drew back automatically revealing a tableau of cartoon characters. We were all a bit flummoxed and various suggestions of who they were flew around the room. To me, they looked like a cross between a Smurf and a Roadrunner. The hotel staff looked as pleased as punch. For the rest of us, it was jaw-dropping disbelief. This was bizarre! I half expected some Redcoat to go on stage and shout 'Hi-di-hi! Welcome to Butlitz'. My musings disappeared and I became very depressed when the food arrived. It was quite the most disgusting food I had ever been served. The Al-Mansour Melia had sister hotels within the group and I made a mental note to never stay at any of them. I can only conclude that someone, somewhere, was on the fiddle. Later in our room, I mentioned how disgusting the food was. Dominic told me to get used to it, as it wasn't going to get any better. He was proved wrong when I later tasted food within Iraq that was wholesome and palatable.

It was now three am and we were told that breakfast was at eight-thirty am. I mentioned that I might well sleep through but Dominic was insistent that I go, 'You must get up. It will be our first chance to meet all the others who are already here. Don't worry, I will wake you.'

I was lying in bed, hoping that we might have a couple of days in the hotel to catch up on rest and a chance to rationalise recent events. I fell into a very deep sleep.

Next morning, after an 'iffy' breakfast of dubious quality, I enjoyed a half pint of good coffee. I recognised some people I vaguely knew from Kuwait. They had been in the hotel for quite some time before our arrival. I spoke to as many as possible trying to gather as much information as I could. Two young men who were with the mother of one of them told me that staff from the British Embassy were arriving later that morning. The mother looked at me, 'They're just children! They will have to fly home with me.'

I looked at the two strapping lads who were over six feet tall, in their late teens and I thought, 'Good luck with that!' We continued to talk for a while but I started to get fed up with her. She was inferring that being put on a strategic site was a death sentence and so, of course, she needed to convince the authorities that the two young men with her were children. As I was shortly to be placed on a strategic site myself, I thought her a trifle tactless. I wandered off gazing at all the scared people clinging to each other. With a shudder, gratitude flooded through me in the knowledge that my wife and child were safe in the UK. In the event that hostilities increased, and who knew when that was going to happen, I was sure to be faced with difficult decisions and was relieved that these could be made without the added pressure of protecting loved ones.

I was adapting to conditions that were extraordinary to me and felt that I was coping quite well, all things considered. To be honest, a few of Saddam's guests were quickly becoming basket cases. After a shower, I sat down at the small coffee table and wrote a letter. It was a 'To Whom It May Concern' type of letter giving power of attorney over my bank accounts which I listed. I also included a personal letter to my wife which was pretty much as you would expect. With an addressed envelope in hand, I returned to the lobby.

A man in a smart, light-coloured, cotton suit was holding court as half-a-dozen Brits hovered around him. Must be Embassy, I thought, as I spotted Colin amongst the throng. 'Hello, there. How are you doing?'

He thrust a sheet of paper into my hand and said, 'Fill that in, will you, old boy? This chap's the Military Attaché.'

I was completing the form with my personal details and comments, when a lady who I later learned was the British Consul, together with a male assistant, entered the hotel and were immediately besieged by their countrymen. I did want to talk to her but thought that I would wait until the initial rush died down.

After twenty minutes or so, I approached her. She was deep in conversation with the woman accompanying the teenagers.

'Sorry to interrupt, but I need to see you and I don't want to miss out if the Iraqis suddenly decide to move me on,' I said.

Her positive response sent me back to the small group where Colin had a concerned look on his face.

'One of the Brits on the bus with us has Hepatitis B. He was sharing the cup of drinking water!'

I was gobsmacked and asked why he hadn't mentioned it and why he hadn't asked for his own cup, which I'm sure could have been arranged. Colin didn't answer. He was as baffled as I was regarding the man's actions. I had been simmering away. I may have looked calm and collected on the outside but inside I was like a pressure cooker. In front of me, talking to the lady consul, was the object of my wrath. I glared at this inconsiderate man and screamed at him, 'You bastard!'

He was lucky there was a lady present!

Both parties stared at me and the consul looked particularly worried. She knew how quickly things could escalate.

'Why didn't you tell us about your Hepatitis? You could have used your own cup instead of sharing. Not very considerate, are you?'

'It's not catching,' he replied. 'I'm ok now – past my contagious period,' he mumbled sheepishly, while avoiding eye contact.

The consul quickly interjected, 'Well, that about wraps it up. I will see you later. I've got to talk to this gentleman now.'

She took my elbow and ushered me to a table in another part of the lobby.

'I'm very sorry. I'm a bit tense with everything and then that guy – well he really got my goat!' I grumbled.

'Yes, it's very difficult for everyone,' she replied.

'Difficult isn't the right word. I've been taken host ... – sorry guest – and that prat decides to keep to himself the fact that he has Hepatitis. Bloody is a better word, I think.' I was still worked up!

She placated me with a smile. 'Have we taken your details?'

'Yeah, and I've given a letter to the military attaché addressed to my wife. It contains details of my bank accounts and gives her power of attorney. It is important that it gets to her.'

'Of course. It will go out in the diplomatic bag.'

The consul looked at me, 'Was there anything else?'

I was in two minds about telling her how we were captured, particularly being blindfolded. Was there any point? My mind made up, I told her and she made notes. She gave me a concerned look. 'Thank you. We really do need to know all these sort of things.'

'Has anyone else been abducted like me?'

'No, this is the first time we have heard of an incident like this one but we don't get to see everyone. Some are in and out before we get access to them.'

'I hope this won't reflect on me with the Iraqis if you are going to make a complaint.'

The consul assured me that the information was for her records only.

I joined a collection of Brits, passed another hour or so, and was just about to return to my room for a nap, when two plain-clothes Iraqis called out for Colin, Patrick and James to come forward. I felt the pit of my stomach churn and went to hear the worst. We were told to pack up and be ready to move. One of the Iraqis took obvious relish from the announcement and I bit my tongue. A feeling of such hatred coursed through my body that I wanted to have a real go at this brainwashed turd! I wanted to tell him what a real hero he was for Jihad. I wanted to tell him he was an amazing frontline trooper and how important it was to organise the placement of civilians on strategic military installations. I wanted to tell him that I thought he was a coward!

I had made some close Arab friends while living in Kuwait and I would meet some decent individuals while being held in Iraq, but at that particular moment I did not hold any kind thoughts for Arabs in general and for Iraqis in particular. I will have to judge each individual on their own merits going forward but at that time, I didn't harbour any feelings of forgiveness for what I was being subjected to.

Colin turned to one of the Iraqis, 'That's all very well but we have to see a doctor first.'

The Iraqis looked puzzled and Colin tried again, 'Look, we have been in contact with someone with Hepatitis. We have to see the doctor on the sixth floor before we can go anywhere. It's all ok, just check with your boss.'

With that he moved towards the lift and both Patrick and I joined him.

'Hello again,' I smiled at Colin.

'This is Patrick, a colleague. I think you briefly saw each other on the bus,' he said.

Patrick smiled and offered his hand which I shook.

The doctor talked to us at some length and concluded that we should be alright. Having talked to the man with Hepatitis, she was satisfied that he was no longer contagious. She said there was very little she could do for the moment. The contagion period was forty days before there were any signs in the blood. She added that if we felt sick when we arrived at Basra airport, we should see a doctor there. We thanked her and left.

We met up again in the lobby but could not see anyone from the Embassy. Colin's delaying tactic at least revealed where we were being taken. We chatted to some Americans that were close by who promised to inform our Embassy, if they could, that the three of us were being taken to Basra airport. I spent a little time trying to find Dominic but to no avail. I had no idea where the man disappeared to. I really didn't want to leave without saying goodbye to a kindred soul who had raised my spirits. I had no choice, of course. I never saw him again.

The three of us boarded an old Iraq Airways bus with two stewardesses and various gentlemen, one of whom spoke very good English and introduced himself as Mr Fawzi. Less than half an hour later we were in a small airport in Baghdad reserved for domestic flights. We were whisked straight onto a plane and for a moment I wondered if the plane was laid on for just the three of us. That was ridiculous, of course, and we were soon joined by hordes of soldiers. They completely filled the plane and we were soon in the air for an hour's flight to Basra, the place we passed through about five hours into our eighteen-hour bus journey!

The flight was uneventful and we touched down at the newly constructed international airport. We were taken to the arrivals hall where the airport manager, a stewardess, Mr Fawzi and five soldiers in uniform who were to be our guards, all sat down to eat lunch together. Following our meal, all of us formed a convoy of just two cars. The soldiers went in one car, everyone else in the other. We travelled within the airport grounds and terminated at a brick-built office block.

Our new accommodation looked well constructed and recently built. We later found that it was built by German contractors. As we got out of the car, I was struck by the fierce heat, and I soaked in the atmosphere of the place. They might have scarred the desert when they built this modern airport but I had to admit that it was very impressive. We were being housed within the service compound and, although there was a steel mesh fence topped by razor-wire, there was little else of a military nature.

Our guards were dressed in civilian clothes with their guns hidden. The airport manager was clearly a decent man trying to make the best of a bad situation. We were shown the shower block which was fifty yards away from our new home and we could see aeroplanes parked close by. During my time at Basra airport I didn't see any activity at all, with the planes remaining idle.

We were taken inside and the circus began. The manager arranged for a table-tennis table to be set up. We all sat down and the stewardess was asked to take notes.

'Do you need anything from the market?'

'What time do you like to eat?'

There were people coming and going all over the place, having a good look at us. We were the first of Saddam's guests to be taken to Basra airport and we were a curiosity. We tried to smile, joke about and generally be pleasant; after all we did not know what was in store for us. With all the furore and staring, I was beginning to feel like a bloody zoo creature. Eventually, everyone barring the guards, left. The guards didn't have much English but showed us to two rooms containing beds. Colin and Patrick shared and – lucky me – I managed to have a room to myself.

13

Detained in Basra

It was late afternoon and I went outside into the oppressive heat. I circled the yard drenched in sweat attracting flies. Thoughts rushed around my head disappearing as quickly as they came: Shit, shit, shit and double shit!

I still couldn't quite understand why I was standing here at this precise time. I did not want to be standing here. Try as I might, I could not stop the negative thoughts or self-pity and was sure that I was going to die. No, that can't be right! We are civilians and on the world stage. Just maybe, the SAS will come and rescue us. It must be a positive that we are at an airport and they could be in with their helicopters with no trouble at all. I tried to calm my brain and reconcile my thoughts. Firstly, the SAS are not coming, that is a given. There are many hundreds of hostages being held against their will on an unknown number of sites. They will have some intelligence but it will not be comprehensive enough to avoid massive casualties.

Remembering my conversations with Dominic regarding our fate, I decided to stop worrying about things over which I have no control. I will try to take things a day at a time. Agonising over what Saddam, Maggie or George might say or do is pointless and will drive me potty. With my newly-found fatalism I pondered possible outcomes to my predicament. I finally settled on three scenarios:

Firstly, the ground war begins and I am blown to smithereens. Secondly – although given the rhetoric a less likely option – a long stay while a protracted negotiated settlement is hammered out. The world is determined that Saddam withdraws from Kuwait which I do not believe is going to happen – Saddam would lose face in the eyes of the Arab world. Finally, Saddam lets us all go before the ground war begins.

With a slightly more positive frame of mind, I decide that if I do get released, I want to be able to walk out with my head held high. Whilst not wanting to antagonise the Iraqis directly, I will be happy to engender a sense of camaraderie at their expense at any given opportunity. I will try to stay positive, not whinge too much, help my pals and treat the Iraqis with disdain. Good! All sorted then. I went back inside and lay down on my bed to have a little chat with God.

I fell asleep and was awoken by Patrick who said that dinner was ready. I took one look and decided you needed to be fairly hungry to consume these provisions. There were cucumbers, tomatoes and dates, which was fair enough, but the hot food looked most unappetising. It was a stew made from okra and tomatoes that was poured into bowls. A bone of some sort of animal was added with the remnants of gristle attached. The concoction was topped with a thick film of grease. With the stew was a roll each and, I kid you not, you could hammer nails in with the thing! I even considered hiding one to use as a club should push come to shove.

We quickly learned that putting the roll in the stew for ten minutes softened it enough to eat without the risk of losing teeth. The food tasted a little better than it looked and I reckoned that, for the time being, we were not going to starve. My spirits dropped as I came to realise that our first evening meal as fully paid up members of the human shield, was the best we were going to get.

'Aren't you going to eat your stew?' Colin asked Patrick.

'I'm not hungry. I think I'll go and lie on my bed,' was the reply.

Our friend was not in a good place. He looked drawn and tense, but then we all did. I felt for him and understood what he was going through but didn't quite know how to help him. I was struggling to keep it together myself. Colin looked at me and nodded towards Patrick's uneaten meal, an unspoken offer to share. I shook my head – I was having enough trouble clearing my own bowl. The food was really beginning to get me down. Forget waterboarding and other forms of torture. Sleep deprivation and shit food will break even the best of men.

The following two weeks were relatively quiet. The US-led coalition were giving their sanctions and trade embargo time to take effect. We all tried to adjust to our predicament in different ways. I often mused that our situation and interaction would be a psychiatrist's dream.

Malcolm, a Brit, along with two Germans, Willie and Alfred, arrived, doubling our complement, which made for a very exciting day. We all got to know each other very well during those endless days of boredom. There were short periods that were very intense in nature, but in the main, mind-torturing monotony was the order of the day.

Distractions of any kind were always welcome and the Iraqis got us excited when they organised a trip into Basra. Hurrah! We were going out; an exciting break to the drudge of the last week or so which we spent trying to come to terms with our dire situation. It was all arranged and the bus was waiting; granted it was only an old beaten up bus but the important thing was that it ran. Dressed in our finest, I think we polished up quite well considering, and anyway, I was fairly sure that there would be no dress code at the Sheraton Hotel restaurant. In any case it was unlikely to be enforced because our dinner companions were all sporting Russian-made Makarov pistols on their hips.

On this surreal evening the first stop was to a museum and Colin and I enjoyed a good chuckle. The displays were akin to a school project. Given the history of the region, this public facility could have been so much better. Moving on, we took an amble along the Shatt al-Arab waterway where a column of statues stood resplendent between the promenade and the river. The bronze depictions of fallen Iraqi heroes, generals and other senior officers, posed with arms outstretched and fingers pointed towards Iran. Colin knew a lot about the military history of the region and, as I read out the name plaques, he commented as to their demise either fallen in the war with Iran or executed by Saddam. Many heroes had indeed faced the executioner. The ideal rank to achieve in the Iraq army under Saddam Hussein's rule was Major. Once promoted above this rank, the officer concerned had a short life expectancy. Saddam regularly culled his senior officers in order to prevent potential coups.

Our evening stroll brought us to the hotel and the maître d' made a great drama out of showing us to our table. The guards'

English was poor and we didn't want to talk to them anyway so we sat in two groups at opposite ends of the table. Menus were brought and the waiter took our order. I do not have a recollection of the fare so can only imagine that it was adequate. However, I do remember the drinks selection! They stocked Heineken which elicited a cheer from me but not so our Colin who was hoping for a good bottle of claret. After protracted negotiations, there was a compromise – he accepted a bottle of Chianti.

The half-litre bottles of lager were going down a treat but the service was slowing after my third. I guess this meal was being provided gratis by the hotel and they were getting concerned by our obvious thirst. This was not my problem; I didn't give two hoots for them so I shouted louder. One of the guards also started yelling at our waiter who scuttled off in double quick time. The beer arrived minutes later and I nodded to my guard who smiled and nodded back. I almost begrudged small kindnesses from the Iraqi military who I wanted to hate and consider the enemy. In reality, the majority I came across did not really like what was happening and certainly hated the detail that they were given.

As the booze flowed, we became louder and more boisterous. Colin was waxing lyrical. He drew us all forward in our seats in a conspiratorial manner as if he was letting us in on a secret, 'Did you know that King Faisal II, King Hussein and Winston Churchill all went to the same school?'

We all laughed and the guards looked on in amusement. Colin spoke with the guards managing to convey that he collected military cap badges and they promised to bring him some. True to their word, by the time we returned to the UK, he had amassed a small collection. Our deliberate time-wasting during dessert, coffee and more booze, could only go on for so long and the soirée came to an end with a jolly bus ride back to our compound. The razor wire-topped fences, locked gates and armed guards were a sobering sight and we were instantly brought back to the reality of our situation.

Standing from left, Willie, Malcolm, an Iraqi gentleman, Jim, Alfred, Colin, another Iraqi gentleman. (*Photo courtesy of Patrick*)

Standing from left, Willie, Patrick, Malcolm, Jim, Alfred, Colin. (*Photo courtesy of Patrick*)

The following morning, I was writing when Willie walked into the room. 'Is that a letter home?' he asked.

'No mate. It's just idle scribbling. I'm having a go at writing some poetry.'

He pulled a grimace and read the effort over my shoulder.

Time Ticks By

Here we are most unusual
Like a broken pendulum;
Sometimes laughingly sad;
Never glad, not really glad.
Not quite alive; just in motion.
Time ticks by for those outside.
Hello we shout! We're inside.
But no one listens, not really.

'It is ok, Jimmy,' was his response.

To everyone I was Jim apart from my brother and father who called me Jimmy. I didn't mind at all that Willie joined them.

'Thanks mate, I really appreciate your enthusiasm.'

I was writing a few notes, poems and letters most days now. It was something to pass the time. The Iraqis managed to find some ruled paper and a couple of pens for me. I was miserly with it and always managed to fit two lines of text for every line on the page. Drawing inspiration from Malcolm who was busy with his daily diary, I tried to keep up, but writing under these circumstances was extremely difficult and there were days when I couldn't concentrate enough to achieve anything at all.

My wife was with her family so I knew she was not going hungry but I was worried that she had not received my power of attorney letter via the embassy in Baghdad. Perhaps the Singapore branch of the MBME bank might still be open. I decided to write another letter and keep it with me at all times in the hope that I might cross paths with someone who could get it out of the country for me.

The General Manager	1 September 1990
MBME Bank	Basra
Singapore Branch	Iraq

Dear Sir,

I apologise for the quality of this handwritten letter but I'm sure you will understand given my circumstances. I have been detained in Iraq at a strategic military installation since 8 September 1990.

I was employed by the Head Office in Kuwait city on a fixed three-year contract between 15 September 1987 and 15 September 1990. I was chief dealer working in the Treasury department.

I had a good relationship with the bank and was asked on a number of occasions to extend my contract, which I declined, solely due to the increased tensions in the area.

My account number is xxxxxxxx. I hope you have current records. I request that the indemnity on my contract be paid by yourselves as my contract with the MBME bank has now expired. I was awaiting settlement from Head Office when Iraq invaded on 2 August 1990.

You will find a claim attached which I believe to be just. I have no calculator or current quotes on air fares, etc. I did receive approximately KD 1,000.00 for annual air fares but that was for the previous year. There will, of course, be an exchange rate discrepancy and I will accept any adjustment you feel should be made, within reason, but I do believe the claim to be accurate.

There is no possibility of communicating with me in the near future. Would you please deal directly with my wife, Mrs A. Payne at the following address: ...

She is authorised to represent me in my financial affairs. Please make any payment, interim or otherwise, to the following account: xxxxxxxx and confirm payment to her.

I enjoyed my time working for the MBME very much and would not hesitate to do so again in Singapore or, indeed, London should it become a full branch.

Yours Sincerely,
J.A. Payne
Currently detained in Iraq

Malcolm provided an envelope. After addressing it to my wife, I wrote a quick note to her and sealed the letter.

We bonded and formed a comradeship that was particular to our strange circumstances. Ridiculous as it may seem, we settled to our fate in Basra. We were uncomfortable with the idea of change – it was all far too unsettling. Better the devil you know and all that! When the Iraqis came and told us that they were splitting us up, we were gutted. Their strategy was to move the hostages round a large number of sites in order to negate any intelligence gathered through the Embassies. We were informed that Willie and Alfred, along with any two Brits were moving to Baghdad. We all wanted to stay together but all the Iraqis could tell us was: 'orders from above'.

I was learning not to dwell on my hunger or fantasies of food but, surely, the grub in Baghdad must be better than the muck we were presently getting. My friendship with Willie, and the humour we developed between us, was a massive help in keeping my spirits up. These were two good reasons that made sense to me and I declared to the group that I wanted to go. Patrick was strongly in favour of staying put and Colin, while being ambivalent about the whole issue, was in favour of staying with his work colleague who had been with him in hiding. That left Malcolm without really a decision to make and, with good grace, he accepted the situation. The guards let us know that we were being replaced with a contingent of Japanese gentlemen. Willie and I looked at Colin and started laughing. Nothing needed to be said.

On 25 September, together with my three friends, we were taken to a domestic terminal where there was the usual chaos with lots of people scurrying about. In amongst the scrum, I could see at least thirty or forty young men in uniform with a pale blue beret. They were instantly recognisable as UN troops. Answering a call of nature brought me into direct contact with one of these guys. We were on our own in the public toilet. 'Do you speak English?' I asked.

'Yes,' He answered.

'I'm a hostage here. Will you take this letter out for me? Maybe the UN has a diplomatic bag.'

'I can't do that,' he said, as he made a brisk exit.

Another UN soldier, looking on and not getting involved!

UN – Ha! Does that mean unelected, unrepresentative or undemocratic? After some time, we boarded a military plane full of Iraqi troops. We were the only four not in uniform. They stared at us but we ignored them. Our no-frills flight landed an hour later and our Baghdad experience began.

14

Detained in Baghdad

On arrival at Saddam International airport we found nothing was prepared. We were on the guest list of the civil aviation authority and a thought crossed my mind that some poor sod was in the shit being blamed for the debacle. Finally, after a few hours of faffing about, we were taken to Gate D41 which was to be our new home. Office partitions were set up to create an area for sleeping and they brought mattresses with bedding that had seen better days. We received a tray of airline food three times a day complete with the plastic cutlery. It may have been destined for economy class but it was good enough to cheer me up!

There were just the four of us and from time to time rumours circulated that others might join our group; it never happened. At very short notice, not that we were exactly settled in, they got us ready to move again. The guards assured us that better accommodation was prepared. We were to travel in two cars with two hostages in each accompanied by our hosts as always. Once again, they insisted on pairing us by nationality. I never understood this aspect of their routine.

After a short drive we approached a compound. The walls were topped with razor-wire. The entrance consisted of a small guard house, barrier and machine-gun nest. My heart dropped to my stomach because this was a completely different level of intensity to Gate D41. We passed under the barrier and watched the soldiers in uniform glare at us. I wasn't aware of the latest propaganda they were subjected to, but they didn't look friendly. A fresh wave of fear was pulsing through the body that I was rapidly losing control of. This was worse than being blindfolded somehow. Maybe a build-up of stress had suddenly popped. Whatever the cause, I wanted to get through it. Taking a deep breath and trying to recall my thoughts of fatalism, I managed to calm myself.

As they walked us round the compound, things were explained. If we were stupid enough to cross the white line painted in front of the actual fuel dump itself, we would be shot. Good to know. You wouldn't want to miss that little titbit of information! We skirted the soldiers at the entrances and, for the first time, we heard the words 'Mamnor' and 'Calaboosh'. The senior amongst them was pointing to the office block. Malcolm gave us a translation: forbidden and prison. 'Mamnor, Calaboosh!' he shouted again, pointing to the fire station. The stores were also a no-go area but we were allowed to walk the compound avoiding the forbidden zones. The abandoned canteen, showers and general recreational area was where we were billeted. This was to be our nightmare existence for an indeterminate time that was ticking ever closer to war.

No fuel tankers ever came to the storage facility during my time at the dump. In fact, it could have been full or empty. Later, I heard a capacity figure of three-hundred million litres being bandied about. The office block was devoid of life and shut up tight as were the stores. The fire station was manned with a skeleton crew. They were not the most energetic bunch of men! The whole place was modern enough and looked like it might be made operational with very little effort but, for the time being, it was on shutdown.

Once inside, and immediately to the right of the entrance to our new quarters, was an office. This was the guards' domain and constantly manned. Lots of people passed through at various times but, on a twenty-four hour basis, it was the guards who were ever present.

A total of four guards lived alongside us – one for every hostage! They worked in pairs, one day on and one day off. The change-over occurred at the same time every day. They had their own dynamic with paranoia going on which we exploited on occasions for our own amusement. We were able to do this because they were from different branches of the regime – one from the military and one from the state police. True to the fear ingrained in the totalitarian regime, they were deeply distrustful of each other. Out of the four, three were ok, indeed one was very decent and likeable. One, however, Abdul, was a complete bastard. The type that comes to the fore in these situations, he took real pleasure in our distress. His sort is seen throughout history and I knew that, if we were to be shot, the other guards would have to be ordered, whereas our resident arsehole would volunteer front line and centre.

The main canteen area became our living quarters. Some of the tables were replaced with sofas and a TV, probably nicked from Kuwait. We possessed a short-wave radio that became a real focus during our stay. The BBC World Service and Deutsche

Welle were the channels of choice. There was a room that resembled a dormitory, a room with a table tennis table and a shower block. Our facilities were certainly no worse than an open prison back in the UK. Here the comparison ended. We were detained for an indeterminate sentence. In fact, if a war started with coalition forces making huge craters with their bombs, it could be a death sentence.

Malcolm was my hero! He woke and slept in a pattern I could only envy. During the day his time was filled with routine. He practiced touch typing, wrote his journal and tried to teach himself to read and write in Arabic. He asked the guards to bring nursery school books of the Jack and Jill variety to support him. Jamal and Fatima was not the same thing at all! Malcolm showed us the books and, yes, they were similar to the Ladybird series except that these books contained stories with tanks and guns. There were drawings of children handling AK47s. When the propaganda starts at kindergarten one despairs for the future of the country. His other daily pastime was running circuits round the office block. The incredible heat and the concrete ground made the gruelling task one of endurance.

There were some old pallets near the stores and we could easily pile them against the wall, throw a mattress over the razor-wire and over we go. A very simple plan that led to some questions. What would the Iraqis be doing while we legged it over the wall? Our hope was either their headless chicken routine or running away. Our next question was when? We decided to go when bombing started – and finally, where would we run to? One of the guys had some experience of Baghdad and believed that he could find the British Embassy. He was certain that we could make it in thirty minutes with a decent pace. Following our escape plan, Alfred told us he wasn't running and that he would take his chances when the time came, but Willie and I joined Malcolm in torturing ourselves.

I had grave reservations about successfully breaking out of the compound and making it to the Embassy but my biggest concern was how to break in. We were all totally convinced that the Embassy would not voluntarily let us in. My experience of them to date left me very pessimistic. All sorts of negative images ran through my mind: one where we are running and a group of Iraqi soldiers open fire but all decide to take aim at the guy with red hair. I needed to banish these thoughts and commit to the plan, rubbish as it was, to keep some glimmer of hope alive, and so every day we pounded the concrete.

Some weeks later, at approximately ten o'clock at night, we heard heavy anti-aircraft fire. The rush of adrenalin was flowing, of course, and I, like the others, wondered if the coalition forces had started bombing. Within a minute, and not enough time for us to exercise even a part of the plan, a dozen armed Iraqi soldiers swarmed all over us. The business end of their rifles were firmly pressed into our chests. The tension was palpable and fear raised its ugly head again. An Iraqi officer entered the room in a relaxed manner and uttered a few sentences. The atmosphere changed in an instant – tension dissipated, rifles were pulled back, and the soldiers' body language relaxed. They started laughing and shuffled out of the room. According to the officer, a young teenager had been a bit twitchy and emptied his magazine when he saw a pigeon.

We were alone again when I asked, 'Do we have a plan B?'

A couple of guffaws rang out but, in the main, we reflected on how vulnerable we were and how the slightest hope in our plan was snuffed out. The following day Malcolm came into the living area. 'Not running today, lads?'

'Fuck that,' said Willie. 'I'm done with the running.'

'Sorry, pal, you're on your own,' I concurred.

Instead of losing a quarter of my body fluids in sweat and dehydrating to the point of exhaustion, I wrote a poem dedicated to the iron man and his determination to run in the heat on concrete in the desert.

Lonely Runner

Across the khaki bank
The blue-grey shimmer of eventide
An autumn haze of clouds and birds
A picture of post card palm trees
And all about seems concrete
With just a hint of life outside.

Loneliness of running around
The concrete under tired feet
In the distance, lonely runner
Sharp against the shimmer
I wonder if he feels the same
That concrete is a killer.

From time to time a daydream of home
Sparked by a thought or the radio
Trying hard to not let go
To keep one's feet on the ground
And all the time I really know
The hatred of that concrete.

Following our move to the compound, the airline food trays were reduced to two per day. When the sanctions started to take effect, the trays disappeared altogether to be replaced with that old favourite, grease stew and hard bread. There was no point in complaining as certain goods were no longer available and because I believed that we were still eating better than the local population.

Three women, two very old and one fifty years younger, made up the cleaning detail. The youngster walked with a distinct limp, evidence that she had survived a bout of polio in early life. The three came twice a week to move the dirt from one spot to another with even dirtier rags. The guards and various others made for a fair number of people with access to our dormitory. Stuff was going missing – there was a thief in the camp!

A senior officer I believed to be a Captain, popped in occasionally and always visited if we asked for him. We decided we wanted to see him about getting a lock fitted to the dormitory. Over coffee we learned that he was a veteran of the Iran-Iraq war and was another soldier not happy with his present duties. He seemed to be a decent man and showed a lot of sympathy with our situation. However, he was very careful about what he said and always looked to see who was in earshot. Before leaving, he told us that we did not need a lock on the door as he would have a word with everyone concerned. I can only imagine that the word was more of a sentence along the lines of 'You will be tortured and killed if you enter their sleeping quarters.' The larceny stopped.

As well as hot food, we received other provisions for the kitchen area, particularly tea and coffee. The coffee and powdered milk came in big commercial tins which we squirrelled away in our newly secure dormitory. We started to hoard. Each hostage received one pack of cigarettes per day, Marlboro to begin with and then, when they ran out, the local brand, Sumer. These contained a small amount of tobacco mixed with wood shavings and other substances that I do not care to mention. Willie and I smoked but the others didn't. We saved the Marlboro as best we could and smoked the Sumer. Cigarettes and coffee always do well as traded goods when the currency is essentially worthless. I was smoking less than ten a day and Willie was trying hard to cut down so we soon accumulated quite a few cartons.

During the majority of October, the radio kept us abreast of the build-up of coalition forces in Saudi Arabia. We heard the rhetoric from Mrs Thatcher threatening war crimes trials – perhaps a bit premature as a war hadn't started yet. The general attitude of the guards cooled a bit and Abdul definitely became even more obnoxious. We were becoming a little feral ourselves, and Willie and I started to really antagonise him. I remember one day in particular when he came into our living area with his condescending sneer so I stared at him and tried not to blink. Shortly, he asked me why I was staring at him. I told him that I wanted to remember his face for the war crimes trial. He bristled and left the room. Very juvenile, I know, but it cheered me up.

The political situation constantly ebbed and flowed and, just as the tension built with posturing of a military nature by both sides, Saddam decided to let all the French hostages go. The decision was aired by the World Service on 22 October and I smiled and was very happy that my Gallic chum, Dominic, might soon be free. Similarly, I was happy for those allowed home in response to the many mercy missions that continued through the early part of November. It surely was a positive that men on the human shield were going home. On the flip side, there were less of us so easier to manage. The women, children, old and sick were all gone now. Younger, fitter men were less of a deterrent and of less use in the propaganda war.

15

A Doctor Visits

The Gulf News and the Gulf Link were both programmes of interest to the human shield. Although similar in name, they could not be more dissimilar in nature. The Link was set up as a Gulf Support Group and was broadcast every day on the BBC World Service. The Germans listened to Deutsche Welle and in the evening we listened to 'Auntie' (nickname for the BBC). Friends and family left messages on tape that were broadcast along with items of interest. One group of hostages was getting messages on a daily basis and Malcolm received a couple himself. I was pissed off that a message hadn't come through for me and it started to play on my mind. We suffered endless hours dwelling on the shit we were in and even the smallest things affected our wellbeing. One day a message came through for me from my wife and I sat right by the radio soaking it all in. Willie knew how hard I was taking being Billy-no-mates and smiled across the room with a big thumbs up. I felt like crying, I was so emotional. I choked back tears and returned the gesture to him with an even bigger smile. This was a hard situation for all of us but would have been a hundred times worse without comrades.

The Gulf News was a programme aired on Iraqi television and broadcast in English. Small groups of the shield were displayed on TV saying how well they were being treated and how their food was tasty and plentiful. On one show I saw two men drinking beer beside a swimming pool! We considered them collaborators. There were hostages who were suffering badly. Hungry Westerners were still hiding in Kuwait, not to mention the Kuwaitis themselves who were being treated appallingly. Any help given to the Iraqi regime by Westerners must be considered traitorous and I hoped they choked on their beer.

An officer visited us and asked if we would like to be on the TV and appear on the 'Guest News'. He was mostly ignored though I did hear one voice telling him to 'fuck off!' Abdul was with the officer and spoke to us, 'You are our guests here in Iraq and should therefore appear on Guest News.'

Even the officer gave him a withering look. Almost losing control and punching Abdul, I jumped out of my seat and grabbed Malcolm's English/Arabic dictionary. I was seething as I pointed out the word 'guest' to Abdul, pushing it towards his face. He grabbed the book out of my hands.

'Read the entry, you idiot! Show me where it says that when you invite someone to be a guest in your home, you have to kick their door down, wave a Kalashnikov at them and drag them into the desert blindfolded! It doesn't, does it? Seems something got lost in translation.'

The officer muttered something about it being difficult for all and they both left. I really hated Abdul!

Willie did his best to calm me down, 'Don't let Abdul upset you, Jimmy.'

'I fucking hate him!' I replied.

'I know, we all do. He's a cockroach. Why don't you use the energy to write one of your poems?'

Abdul is a prick
I hate him with all my being
I want to stick a pickaxe in his head ...

Only joking – I would not waste my precious paper on that piece of slime.

Sanity Drifting

Into the soul
Searching for strength
Deeper and deeper
With desperation
Time is oppressive
All seems against you
Sanity drifting
Paranoid thoughts.

What can we do?
Each fibre screaming
Give us our freedom!
Give us some hope!

Holding us back
Tainting our spirit
Politeness and niceness
So patronising

Temper our hate
Bitterness over
Let us go home!
Then we'll forgive you.

What can we do?
Each fibre screaming
Give us our freedom!
Give us some hope!

Hapless and helpless
All of our feelings
Held within us
Held with our freedom
Each day is hopeless
Each week is endless
Listen to us
Let us go home!

What can we do?
Each fibre screaming
Give us our freedom!
Give us some hope!

Anything to break the monotony of guest life was welcome. Willie was not particularly religious as far as I knew but decided that he wanted to go to church. He asked Mohammad, one of the less officious guards, if it could be arranged. Mohammad went to telephone the Captain and disappeared into the office. This was not a ridiculous request given that the Christian population of Iraq was in excess of one and a half million. This meant that there were churches and cathedrals in the capital. Abdul came flying out of the office and approached Willie. 'The orders are to stay here. You're not allowed to leave the compound.'

'Fuck off!' was the only response he got.

An hour later, the Captain arrived and listened to Willie's request. He did not think it possible. My pal was not ready to concede and gave an eloquent argument. He expressed his respect for the rights of each individual to worship in their own way. The guards and everyone else working here were entitled to go to the mosque. As we were guests of Saddam, surely he would want us to be happy and able to pray? The Captain raised his eyebrows and smiled. He was a perceptive fellow and knew that the request was probably more from boredom and mischief than any religious calling. He reported that he would try his best, and off he went.

A few days later he told us that leaving the camp under any circumstances was 'Mamnor'. However, he had arranged for an Archbishop to visit the following Thursday. I looked on at the Captain's frustration with Willie's complete lack of enthusiasm. Clearly he was more interested in some time outside the camp than any act of contrition.

The Iraqi regime allowed us to send letters home and promised that they would be delivered. As we didn't receive anything in reply, we jumped to the conclusion that the Iraqis were in fact bullshitting us. Consequently, we had all written letters that we hoped the Archbishop might somehow deliver to our homes.

I was sitting at one of the tables scribbling a few notes when the Archbishop arrived. His robes were a stunning white decorated with beautiful embroidery. I went to get Willie who always stayed in bed for most of the morning.

'Willie, the Archbishop is here. Don't forget the letters.'

I made my way back and sat facing the Archbishop.

'Can I be of any help to you?' he said.

'I'm not a Catholic.'

'That doesn't matter. We're all Christians. God makes no distinction,' said the man dressed in white.

We chatted about the situation but he had no new information, or at least any that he was prepared to discuss, and I lost interest. His persona did radiate goodness and he seemed eminently suited to his calling. Willie joined and introduced himself. They walked the twenty or so yards to a canteen table at the other end of the room. Turning side on, with an open palm shielding their eye lines, they set themselves for confession. I saw my friend reach under his shirt for the letters and then stop and remove his hand. He rose and returned to the sitting area. The priest made a little chit-chat and left.

'How did it go?' I asked.

'He might be a Christian, but he is an Iraqi first!'

I thought my friend was a trifle harsh as the Archbishop had given his word to the Captain that he wouldn't bring anything to us or take anything from us. This was to be the Archbishop's one and only visit.

Three months had passed since the invasion. October turned into November and the temperature dropped, particularly at night. Over the last month there was a massive build-up of forces in Saudi Arabia and many mercy missions from people such as Ted Heath and Tony Benn. The press nicknamed them the grovelers – they certainly were made to kiss Saddam's arse in order to take any hostages home with them. The Iraqi regime displayed a growing antipathy for the USA and the UK so I knew there was to be no mercy for me. I was going nowhere! The shortages became more noticeable and Guest News reported the guests were receiving the same rations as the Iraqi people. On the TV I noticed Saddam smoking a fat cigar so clearly not all of the people.

The political and military stance of the West hardened during October. The rhetoric was cranked up and the attitude of our guards cooled further. As they became more familiar with us, contempt replaced false politeness. We, in turn, were more feral and fatalistic making no effort to hide our disdain of them. We suffered our isolation and fear each and every day but, of course, some days were better than others. On the most special of days, those as rare as hens' teeth, the whole horrible scenario was pushed to the back of our minds and, just for a short while, we felt normal.

Saturday 3 November was just such a day when the Captain asked us to provide telephone numbers as we were all permitted to call home. Malcolm came out of the office grinning from ear to ear having just talked to his family. He looked ten years younger. My turn, and I was so excited! The guards dialled the number and left the office. The phone rang and rang but no one answered. Tremendous! My wife was out. This particular Saturday really was one of rarest of days – Willie and Alfred were given parcels via the German Embassy and were told that they would be able to receive letters from home. Abdul made a great show of bringing the parcels and then saying to me, 'Nothing for you. Me-sees Tatcher is very bad!'

'Fuck off!' – by then my standard response to Abdul.

The phone calls home came just at the right time. Tension was building and we were collectively struggling to stay positive. It was a relief to know that we were not forgotten back home and that many people were working hard on our behalf.

There was a belief amongst the Iraqis that if a guest died, then so would all the people looking after him. When one of our guys complained of chest pains, all the Iraqis in the camp went into overdrive. A doctor was brought to assess the need for the guest to go to hospital. Once it was established that he was suffering from severe indigestion which didn't surprise me in the least, given the quality of some of the food, they stopped panicking and the tense atmosphere calmed a little. The Iraqis decided that we should avail ourselves of this opportunity and told us to see the doctor in turn. This was the second time that I consulted with a doctor in Iraq and both times the doctors were female.

At the time Iraq was a little different to its neighbours when it came to the structure of their society. The country took a more liberal stance on religion and women compared with the rest of the Arab world. The majority worshipped Allah but, in a country of eighteen million, ten percent were Christian and there was a community of around three hundred thousand Arabs who followed the Jewish faith. Women enjoyed a degree of autonomy and were certainly well represented in the medical profession. My experience of the men was that they were bone idle and I believed that the freedom that the women enjoyed, was born out of necessity rather than any sense of moral compass.

The Iraqis were living in fear just as in all totalitarian regimes. Stalin provided the blueprint for the Ba'ath party structure.

The paranoia was at ridiculous levels with even the most intelligent citizens not thinking clearly. Willie came out of the office where the doctor commandeered the desk and told me it was my turn. I entered and looked at the woman who I guessed to be in her mid-forties. Although she was stern looking, she was attractive with a good figure and an excellent command of English. There was nothing wrong with me but I was happy enough to sit there and while away a little time.

'Good afternoon, James. I am the resident doctor at the airport.'

'Good afternoon. My name is Jim. No one calls me James.'

'Fine. So, Jim, how is everything?'

'As well as can be expected considering I'm sitting on three-hundred million litres of aviation fuel and a war is about to start,' I replied with a smile.

Although she maintained her severe expression, I thought I caught just the faintest of cracks in the corner of her mouth as a smile started to form.

'Is there anything I can get for you?' asked the doctor.

'Something for depression would be nice.'

There was a full-blown smile now and a twinkle in her eye. With a chuckle she replied, 'Well, if you can suggest something for me ... '

As quick as the words popped out of her mouth, the smile disappeared and fear crept into her eyes. Paranoia was raising its ugly head again and I wondered if she might be worried that the room was bugged and that she had compromised herself in the conversation she was having with 'the guest'. This was another instance when I felt some sympathy for the civilian population.

The doctor passed me a small bag containing twenty or so small tablets the size of sweeteners. 'These are valium. They should help with your anxiety.'

I thanked her and returned to our quarters where I swallowed two of the tablets. After one hour had passed, I took two more, and two more an hour after that. Deciding they were, in fact, sweeteners, the rest went into the bin.

16
Letter to Saddam

We had long since read the few books the guards brought us and our constant requests for new material fell on deaf ears – either they were not available or our minders just didn't care. The table tennis table was used daily and my match-ups with Willie were the most enjoyable as we were of a similar standard. 'Pingers, Jimmy?' was a question I heard so many times. I had mentioned how we called table tennis 'Pingers' at school, a derivation of ping pong. Willie took to the term like a duck to water.

Backgammon was the other game that became a daily staple. The guards gave us a shallow wooden box filled with plastic counters that were white and a shade of green. When opened, the box doubled as the board. There were no triangular markings on the rough wood but there were semi-circular indentations indicating where the column of counters should be. I played with whoever wanted a game and, when there were no takers, I hassled Malcolm or Willie into playing.

I spent hours and hours on that board and found myself winning more often than not. Word must have made it to the fire house where there was a backgammon player who fancied himself as Omar Sharif. Mohammad asked if I would like to play with the men from the fire station, to which I had no objections. These were just regular guys, non-military, and anyway, I wanted to improve my play and any break in the monotony was also most welcome. That evening four of the guys from the fire house came in with big smiles and introduced themselves.

Not one of them spoke English so Mohammad acted as interpreter. When the guys produced a few litre bottles of beer, our guard got a bit flustered but decided to turn a blind eye. The game was underway and I was a bit merry when the suggestion of a wager was put forward. I expected their main man to turn it on and hustle me out of our cigarettes. My glass was re-filled and I smiled. They were trying to get me pissed to gain an advantage and, without a second thought, I was going to let them.

We decided the ante would be one pack of Sumer cigarettes and I was not particularly bothered if we lost a few packs because we had amassed over ten cartons in our hoard. As I had been alcohol free for some time, the beer began to take effect and I was enjoying myself, lost in the moment instead of the constant worry. Our language barrier proved a hit when I started using every Arabic swear word in my limited vocabulary each time I threw rubbish dice. They laughed at my pronunciation when I berated the dice for being gawads (pimps) and worse.

The evening was ours as double sixes flowed and it was close to midnight when the guys made their farewells with promises to repeat the evening. We were a carton of smokes to the good. I pulled Mohammad aside and asked if the firemen would like to trade. We wanted beer and I suggested Marlboro as our barter instead of using the commercial quantities of coffee and powdered milk we also possessed. I didn't want the Iraqis to confiscate our supplies. The guards knew that with non-smokers among us we were likely to have a store of cigarettes.

The evening was enjoyable but, unfortunately it was not to be repeated. Mohammad was cagy and skirted the subject and I never saw the firemen again. I wondered if Abdul had got wind of it and made a report. I really, really did hate that guy.

Willie and Alfred shared their parcels with Malcolm and me, all except for the paperback books in German. Imagine that – the German Embassy were able to bring such luxuries to Baghdad! It was not just the books, toothpaste and other items, it was the food, a welcome supplement to the rations. The food was in tin foil containers that could be heated in a decent sized kettle. These parcels were arriving weekly together with letters from home.

Malcolm and I waited for any sort of contact from the Embassy or at least a message over the Gulf Link on the World Service. If they had explained that they had tried but failed due to the hatred of the regime for Margaret Thatcher, or that they had tried and failed because the Iraqis were attempting to break us through 'divide and rule', with largesse showered on the Germans and meanness shown to the English, then fair enough. No, that was not it. That was just paranoia creeping in. I have it now – they just do not care!

I believed British Embassies were concerned with a number of activities. They worked with spies, promoted British interests and they housed a commercial section focused on British exports. Other countries' embassies viewed the welfare of their citizens as a priority. When a fellow countryman encountered difficulties they were quick to help. On the other hand, British Embassies regarded any of their citizens in trouble as nuisances. They considered this part of their job remit as tiresome. I sympathised when it came to dealing with lager louts on the piss in Spain, behaving disgracefully and then expecting the full repatriation service. Au contraire, we were hard-working family men who were incarcerated through no fault of our own. We were, in effect, a British export.

'What are you writing?' Willie asked.

'Just a quick note to my Embassy. If I give it to Mohammad, there is a miniscule chance that they'll receive it.'

The British Embassy

Dear Fellow Countrymen,

I am currently a guest in Iraq with a fellow countryman, Mr xxxxx. We reside with two German citizens and they are receiving one crate of supplies each per week along with letters from home.

I realise that you are probably extremely busy but a short note explaining why we cannot receive letters would put our minds at rest. The attitude of the Iraqi administration seems to be easing and we can now make phone calls. We have been informed that we can receive goods from yourselves.

I would appreciate if you could send me some paperback novels together with some alcohol, preferably a couple of bottles of scotch and a few crates of beer.

If the government cannot buy me a drink during my sad predicament, then I can supply the name and address of a private citizen countryman who will be happy to foot the bill as I am sure the British government considers me a bad credit risk at the present moment in time.

Furthermore, the Iraqis have advised us that our personal belongings can be collected from our residencies in Kuwait. However, they cannot advise us what will happen to our belongings, whether shipped to the UK, placed in storage in Baghdad, or stolen en route.

Please investigate this initiative and outline its full implications. I eagerly await your reply,

Yours sincerely,
J.A. Payne
Guest of Iraq

We were allowed to make one call home per day, which was a dream come true initially. The calls allowed us to reconnect with our families and confirm that we hadn't been forgotten. Malcolm, in particular, quickly found them an essential part of his existence and I worried for his wellbeing should they suddenly cease. For me personally, I had mixed feelings. At first when I got through to my wife, I was ecstatic to hear all the news and well wishes from home. After a week or so, I found the conversations a little difficult because there was very little from my side that I wanted to divulge and my wife had brought me up to date with life at home. She was staying in a lot glued to the news on the TV so didn't have a vast amount to tell me. We were both a bit frustrated with the situation although I never tired of hearing updates about our daughter Charlotte who was eighteen months old when I last saw her. She would be two years old in mid January and I hoped with all my might that I would be home for her party.

The guards took us into the office, made the connection and left us in privacy. One day, while making a call, I noticed some files on the desk. I took a sneaky peek and guessed them to be personnel files. I had no idea why someone forgot to lock the files away but I was not going to miss this opportunity. In the top right-hand corner was a photograph. I nearly exploded with glee when I found Abdul's file. Although in Arabic, it was not that different in layout compared with similar records in English.

Close by the photograph was a box containing script and numerals, the only part of the file that looked like an address. During the rest of the call Mandy did not receive my full attention. I took a scrap of paper from the bin and made a copy of the address as best I could. Later I checked with a friend and it was indeed an address and my copy was legible. Quite what I was going to do with the information was not clear at that time but I felt that it might come in handy.

November seemed endless and war an inevitability. The month proved to be the hardest yet. Because the women, children, old and sick were all gone now, the media coverage dropped away. Shortages were more common which meant that the quantity and quality of rations dropped significantly. Activity at the end of this dreadful month suddenly took off. On 29 November the United Nations Security Council (UNSC) finally made a decision authorising the use of force to expel Iraq's occupying army from Kuwait. They settled on 15 January 1991 as the deadline for withdrawal. The following day, 30 November, George Bush invited Saddam to engage in direct talks.

At times we found it difficult to analyse news items objectively because we were too close to the situation. When the UN news came through, the icy fingers of fear ran up and down my spine. The ticking time bomb was activated and, although scared, I was almost relieved that the endless wait would soon be over one way or the other.

During November we were asked if we wanted to invite our wives to come to Iraq for Christmas. They were to meet with Saddam and request that their husbands return home with them. This horrible piece of propaganda was torture for me. The idea of placing my family at risk and taking part in the charade chilled me to the core but a small selfish part of me was whispering in my ear – what is the harm? A couple of days of nonsense and then I could be home! No one from our group took up the offer and, during my next call I told my wife, no matter how she felt, not to travel to Iraq. She was considering the initiative but, with some persuasion, agreed not to come.

What started as a shitty month, grew into a torturous one and then ended full of action. The Germans were allowed to leave and, although I was extremely happy for them, I knew that I was going to miss Willie. His humour was a good match with mine and he had prevented me from drifting into deep depression on many occasions. I would miss Alfred as well but we did not have such a firm relationship due to the language barrier – his English was ok but conversation was difficult and my German was non-existent.

Within two days of Willie's departure, one of the gate guards he had bribed, came to our accommodation with a big parcel. He had gone to the market and managed to buy some paperback novels, chocolate, beer, whisky and other, much appreciated luxuries. He was a star and I owed him. Hot on his heels, the Embassy also made a delivery. Sitting outside the office were two huge duffle bags. They were attached to two foot square pieces of wood with castor wheels. I had never seen anything quite like it – three times the size of the package that Willie sent us. We fell on them like kids at Christmas! The contents were pitiful: two parka coats made in China that neither of us could actually get on comfortably, the sleeves barely reaching our elbows; two packets of powdered soup; three novels in a dilapidated state, missing pages and all of them of the Barbara Cartland variety; and half a copy of a *Cosmopolitan* magazine dated five years earlier.

Given that this was the only contact made in three months, we were beyond disappointment and I was fuming! This was an insult. They would have been better off doing nothing at all. We returned to our living area both moaning away. One of the guards asked us to take the parcels and we told him that we didn't want them. He produced a chit and asked us to sign our receipt. I could not believe it and told the guard to return the parcels with the chit unsigned. The Germans were not subject to such red tape and their goodies were worth pinching! It is coming – someone from the Embassy is going to get it with both barrels. I wonder who it will be?

A group of women arrived from the UK and, after kissing Saddam's arse, secured the release of their husbands. Our Captain visited again, emphasised how smoothly things had gone with no danger and asked us to reconsider and invite our wives for Christmas. We were still not interested but, on a whim, I asked if I could write to Saddam.

'Of course. Saddam is very interested in his guests' wellbeing and the letter will be delivered today if you write it now.'

Saddam Hussein	Saddam Hussein
President of Iraq	International Airport
	1 December 1990

Dear Sir,

For the love of God please let us go home to our families for Christmas.

Yours sincerely,
J.A. Payne
A Guest

Malcolm was looking over my shoulder and his sniggers turned into a belly laugh: 'There is no way that letter will get to Saddam.'

'It might do. The Captain said it would,' I countered.

He wandered off in hysterics, 'That will be in the first bin the Captain passes.'

Unbeknownst to us, things were moving at a pace. On 4 December Saddam met with Yasser Arafat and King Hussein of Jordan. Both leaders urged Saddam to release the human shield and allow non-nationals to exit the country. The world had condemned the use of hostages and, by releasing us, he might garner support amongst the growing movement in the West that was opposed to conflict. They believed an avenue of dialogue with King Fah'd of Saudi Arabia might lead to a settlement between Iraq and Kuwait with regards to the disputed islands and the Al-Rumeilah oil field.

Although the UNSC passed a mandate sanctioning the use of force, no sanction was given for an invasion of Iraq. Our continued detainment might well muddy the waters and give the coalition reason to enter. The situation was confusing and fluid, changing almost hourly. Whatever or whoever influenced Saddam to come to the decision to release us, had my unreserved gratitude. This momentous announcement took place on 6 December 1990. Malcolm and I were listening to the World Service when we heard the great news. We started jumping up and down and hugging each other. I looked him in the eye and said, 'He got my letter then!'

17

Al-Mansour Melia Hotel Part 2

The waiting was dreadful during the last few days of captivity. The clock could not tick round fast enough. Abdul's attempts to make friends with Willie before he left were met with utter disdain and now he was trying to ingratiate himself with us. The plan to move us from a site very close to the airport, to the Al-Mansour Melia Hotel and then back to the airport, seemed counter-productive to me. The Iraqis could complete their red tape and return our passports at check in. Apparently, I was still not in charge of my own destiny and so I played my part in the media circus at the 'freak show' hotel in full view of the world's press.

Mohammad told us to be ready to leave the following morning – 9 December. I took the opportunity to have a quiet word with him.

'Make sure that you are working when we leave. You can tell the captain that you want to say goodbye. Let him know that we do not want Abdul around when we leave.'

Mohammad nodded and went to the office. I was enjoying a cup of tea when Abdul interrupted my happy reverie, 'Mr Jim.

I will bring a barber. You can have a shave and haircut to look good for the cameras and your family.'

I loved the way that he started to call us 'Mr' and address us cordially since it became clear that we were leaving. At the start of this whole ordeal, Martin and I decided that we wouldn't shave or cut our hair until we were home. A stupid deal struck after a few drinks.

'No, Abdul. That won't be necessary. I'm not going to cut my hair or my beard.'

'Then you will have to stay here. We can't let you go to the hotel looking like that.'

'Fine! I will stay here. It is very cheap to live as a guest of Iraq.'

The clock finally ticked round to 9 December and we were packed and ready to go. I drank one last cup of coffee and penned another poem. I might never become the Poet Laureate but the poems and other scribbles kept me occupied.

Any Day Now

Waiting; mind promising
Not long now
Sitting; thinking surely
Any hour.

Tap dripping
Time tormenting
The rhythm flow
Of waiting.

Watch ticking
Fridge humming
Sitting; thinking maybe
Any day now.

Mohammad informed us that the transport had arrived. We took him to our dorm and I told him in no uncertain terms that he was not to share with Abdul, not one single cigarette. He hated the man almost as much as we did and was adamant that he was not getting anything. The hoard was quite substantial, mainly cigarettes, coffee and powdered milk. He looked on in amazement. 'There are more goods here than in the shops.'

Mohammad was wide eyed as I shook his hand goodbye. Both he and his colleague could significantly supplement their wages with the proceeds from our supplies. He asked me to wait and quickly ran to the sitting area. He returned with the backgammon set, 'Please take this, Jim. I think the board is for you now.'

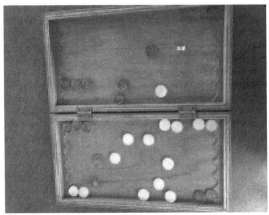

The Backgammon Set.

Having played on it for many hours, I was quite touched.

Two four-wheel drives were sent to carry us to the hotel. Three soldiers travelled with Malcolm and I in one car and another five soldiers in the car following. They were worried that the Iraqi people so incensed with seeing Westerners, might rip us limb from limb. We reached a major roundabout and were trapped in complete gridlock. The soldiers were angry, gesticulating and shouting at all the drivers within range. Waving their rifles about, they scared the pants off them but it didn't help because for the moment, the cars were not going anywhere.

An Iraqi gentleman, probably in his late twenties, saw us from the pavement and approached the car. Immediately one of our soldiers started shouting and waving his rifle around. The man ignored the soldier completely and, looking me in the eye, said, 'I am Christian like you.'

It did not seem appropriate somehow to get into a philosophical discussion with this chap regarding my beliefs. The soldier poked him with the barrel of his rifle and shouted some more. The man took a packet of cigarettes and started passing me some through the car window. He never once looked at the soldier. He ignored him as if he didn't exist. I thanked him and wished that he would just go. There was never a question in my mind that he might well be shot at any moment. With a smile and a hand patting his chest above his heart, he repeated, 'I am Christian like you', and with that he walked off.

This small act of courage and defiance convinced me that not all the population could be broken and subjugated. At the roundabout we encountered indifference with some mild curiosity but, certainly, no one seemed interested in ripping us limb from limb. Somehow the traffic unclogged itself and we were on the move. In no time at all we pulled up outside the Al-Mansour Melia Hotel. Maybe I should apply for a loyalty card as this was my second stay in three months.

We entered the reception area and my senses were overloaded with the carry on. Lights and cameras were everywhere with hundreds of people milling around. The noise and close proximity of so many people shook me up and, looking at Malcolm, I could see that he felt the same. 'Jesus. Look at this lot,' he said.

The soldiers pushed through the scrum and discharged their duty as soon as we were registered and given a room key. It was easy to guess which men came from the sites because we all carried a haggard, gaunt look. The accumulation of stress and weight loss had taken a toll on our bodies. I, myself, was two and a half stone lighter than I was on the day of invasion.

Malcolm was collecting the key when a reporter with microphone and recording equipment asked me if we had just come from a site.

'Yes. We were on an aviation fuel dump.'

'I'm from a radio station in London and I want to interview some of the hostages.'

I had never heard of the channel before.

'I'll conduct a live interview but it will be aired in the UK tomorrow.'

'What sort of time will it be aired?' I asked.

'It's planned for the six-thirty am slot tomorrow morning.'

I thought that the chances of anyone I knew listening to that channel at six-thirty am on a Monday morning were slim.

'Ok. I'll do it for a bottle of scotch and a carton of Marlboro.'

'There are over five hundred Brits here all ready to talk their heads off for free,' he said.

'Well, best you go and speak to them then and stop wasting my fucking time.'

Malcolm and I took the lift to our room and dropped our bags. We were told to collect our passports from an area set aside in reception and were on our way to pick them up. The lift was packed during our descent and I was still suffering from the sensory overload. The doors opened at the mezzanine floor and I jumped out. 'I'll walk down from here and catch you up.'

He gave me a nod. Having dealt with the feeling of claustrophobia, I placed my hands on the guard rail and watched the chaos in the lobby below. Camera crews and the usual media circus were gathered amongst Embassy personnel and, of course, the 'honoured guests'. Adjacent to me were two men in conversation. I overheard the gentleman in a suit telling the other man that he would fly home with the British and be met at Heathrow airport, taken to a hotel and then flown on to Malta the following day. I waited for a lull and intervened, 'Excuse me. I'm sorry to interrupt but are you anything to do with the Maltese Embassy?'

'I am the Maltese Ambassador,' replied the man in the suit.

'Would you spare me five minutes when you've finished with this gentleman, please?' I asked.

'We're done, I think. Unless there is anything else I can help you with?'

The Ambassador raised his eyebrows towards his countryman who shook his hand, thanked him and wandered off.

'How can I help you?' asked the diplomat.

I felt a little ridiculous asking. I mean, why should he know my friend just because he is a Maltese citizen? Ray is larger than life, however, and there cannot be that many Maltese in the region. 'I was hoping you might have news of my friend. He is Maltese and his name is Ray.'

'You're Jim Payne,' he said smiling.

I was gobsmacked. With the wind taken out of my sails, I said, 'My God! Is he here in Baghdad?'

'Do you know your friend has asked me if I could find some information about you – where you were taken and how you were being treated? He has sent weekly faxes and people coming from Kuwait drop into my office from time to time with messages from your friend. I contacted your Embassy. They were not very helpful but I passed on the little information I did get to Ray.'

With a grin like a Cheshire cat, I listened while the Ambassador brought me up to date with the reports he had received. Ray was helping to move people in hiding amongst a variety of villas and apartments he had keys for. News was craved by all and he made televisions available and vehicles where necessary. The Ambassador was not sure if he was going to leave Kuwait before the ground war started or whether he would stay the distance.

Two years following the conflict when things were returning to normal, Martin, Ray and I met in a bar in Bahrain. Ray told us that after the fighting was over he started to have more and more contact with the American forces that ousted the Iraqis. He spotted a chance to make some money. During the invasion he had amassed a large number of twenty-five Iraqi dinar notes, the ones with a picture of Saddam Hussein's head. The Iraqi dinar was now worth very little as a currency but as a souvenir to an American GI, it was worth fifty US dollars. He also acquired a container load of quality t-shirts. He printed them with various liberation themes of a humorous nature. At a huge mark-up, the troops lapped them up.

The fleeing Iraqis set fire to the oil wells in the country and the buildings in the city were in a dreadful state with tar-like deposits from the fires exacerbating the dilapidation already caused. This provided Ray with another opportunity. He was talking with a group of displaced manual workers mostly from the Philippines and the subcontinent. They were scared and hungry. He decided to accommodate them, feed them and supply them with cleaning materials. He put them back in employment cleaning the larger, more luxurious villas to which he had access. These guys were so happy. The Americans were keen to secure accommodation for their senior officers. Ray supplied them and cleaned up both literally and figuratively. I consider my shrewd friend to be a bit of a hero who helped a good many people during those difficult times.

Malcolm was not easy to spot in amongst the chaos so I joined the queue to retrieve my passport. While scanning the crowd, I caught sight of Peter, a good friend from Kuwait. Our last contact took place before the invasion.

'Jim!' he screamed across the lobby and came striding towards me.

He temporarily silenced the throng but the babble returned by the time he reached me. We hugged and smiled at each other. Peter was another extraordinary character whose zest for life made him very likeable. He was one of the best foreign exchange dealers I ever encountered and he was also as mad as a bag of frogs. He related his own experience since the invasion and we swapped our most unpleasant experiences like old soldiers comparing battle scars. He was near the docks area within days of the invasion and decided to take some photos of the tanks and soldiers to show to his teenage sons who were back in the UK. The Iraqis grabbed him and, during interrogation, accused him of being a spy. Peter said that it was probably a stupid thing to do in hindsight.

'You think!? In hindsight!? A stupid thing to do!?' I was struggling to get the words out through my laughter.

He was suffering with a bad back but otherwise appeared in reasonable shape. However, he did tell me how they dragged him out of bed at three o'clock in the morning, put him up against a wall and, with a mock firing squad, discharged blanks at him. To push the Iraqis to take such a step, he must have been an absolute pain in the backside and I loved him for it. As I was next in line, we finished our conversation and promised to meet up in the bar.

My passport was returned and, although not back in the UK yet, I did feel liberated. The radio reporter returned. 'You're one of the few men who told me to fuck off. I think you might be worth interviewing. I wasn't able to get whisky or Marlboro but I managed a bottle of arak [a drink similar to ouzo] and a carton of Sumer.'

Arak was a favourite of mine. 'Ok, no problem. I'll take the arak but I'm not bothered about the fags.'

The arak was in his room so we decided to conduct the interview there. Less than an hour later, I left his room with a half bottle of arak – good job radio chap was teetotal while working. When I met up with my brother and a friend back in London, they both said that they heard me on the radio. I was flabbergasted and asked how the interview was. They both reported difficulty in following as every other word was bleeped over.

18

Flight from Baghdad

On my return to the lobby, the chaos reached another level making my task of catching up with Malcolm even harder. Considering we had just spent three months almost constantly in each other's company, maybe I should leave him to it. I abandoned my search and soaked up the atmosphere. The relaxing of tension, together with the half bottle of arak, left a warm buzz and I was smiling away to myself.

A slender young man tapped me on the shoulder, 'Excuse me, have you just arrived from a site?'

'A few hours ago,' I replied.

'I work at the Embassy. Have you registered with us yet?'

My smile increased and a shiver of pleasure ran through me. Here was the person who was going to get it purely because he represented the British Embassy. Although I believed myself to be in good shape, I clearly had lost my sense of reason.

'My name is Jim Payne. Can you please help me? I don't think that I can manage on my own.'

The feeling amongst the men returning from the sites was similar to my own. The Embassy had not done enough for us.

So far they had taken my name and sent me a parcel that was a cruel joke. The delivery was huge in size but contained absolutely nothing of any use whatsoever. Now, for my third contact, they wanted to take my name again! The Embassy employee was happy to be of use rather than the subject of veiled abuse and led me to their desk. We completed the necessary as we chatted away, 'I don't have a single dinar. Do you think you could buy me a drink at the bar? I have been dreaming of an ice cold beer for a long time now.'

There were no objections so off we went to the bar. As I was enjoying the cold beer, I noticed a man at a table close by. He didn't have a drink in front of him. I caught his eye, 'British?'

'Yes, mate. I was just brought here today,' he replied.

'Have you any cash?'

He shook his head.

'Come and have a drink with us. My new friend here is buying.'

The man joined us and another round was ordered. Two more guys were passing, 'British?'

'Yes mate,' said one of them.

'Come and join us. This kind man from the Embassy is buying the drinks.'

My new-found friend paid the barman and told us that he really must go because he had work to be getting on with. With a vice-like grip I put my arm round his shoulders, 'Sorry, pal, but we haven't finished drinking yet. Surely the Embassy can pick up the bar tab just this once?'

He sighed and gave me a resigned look. He took out his wallet and placed his money on the bar with good grace and left. A group of six of us took an hour to spend his money.

My brain was not functioning on all cylinders as I now thought that I was square with the Embassy. They had insulted me with the so-called care package which should have been called the 'we don't care' package but now, because they had bought me a drink by way of apology, all was forgiven.

The rest of the evening was a bit hazy but I remember still being in the bar when they brought the shutters down. The guys were getting very rowdy and things looked like they might get out of hand. A couple of chaps made a foray into the kitchen and returned with a few cases of beer to a huge cheer and we carried on quaffing. Thankfully Malcolm had wedged our room door open although I am sure that I probably disturbed him.

The next day, 10 December, with a horrendous hangover tempered by euphoria, I was again taken to Saddam Hussein International Airport where the Iraqi propaganda ministry eked out the last vestige of our usefulness. We queued at passport control and a camera crew approached us.

'I'm Jeremy Bowen from the BBC. Could we interview you, please?'

My five minutes diatribe was never going to be aired, but Malcolm who followed me spoke coherently and with a great deal of intelligence. One of the crew made a note of our names and then moved on. A few days later I caught our departure from Iraq on the news. Sure enough, Malcolm's interview appeared on the TV, but with my name subtitled across his chest.

As we came closer to passport control, we could hear the thump as the official banged his stamp onto an ink pad, followed by a passport. He had a rhythm going and, for a horrible moment, I felt the urge to grab the stamp and make an impression on his forehead. With juvenile urges suppressed, I passed through to the departure lounge and took a look at the stamp: EXIT IRAQ 10/12/1990. Exit stamps were usually located beside entry stamps which together were close to the visa. The stamp in my passport was all on its own centrally located on a blank page. So where were the visa and entry stamps then? Oh yeah! I remember – they don't exist because I was kidnapped and taken into the country against my will!

The hours passed as we sat in the departure lounge watching various nationalities board their planes. I must have nodded off and I awoke with a feeling of dread because just for a split second I imagined that I was back at Gate D41.

The planes were chartered from Iraq Airways at a huge premium. Rumours were rife and, of course, my favourite involved Mrs Thatcher. There were 540 of us, just too many for one plane. The story was that Maggie requested the first and business class seats to be replaced by second class so that we could all travel home together on the one plane. You could not make this stuff up although someone must have! I thought the speculation regarding our number was not a bad guess but as to the rest – well, it made for a good story.

The day passed into evening when a hubbub of excitement rippled through the crowd. It was time to board. I was placing my bag in an overhead locker when Khalid, aka Brian from the bank, jumped into my window seat, 'Christ, where did you come from?'

At the same time I noticed two Iraqi soldiers in the aisle, 'Khalid, you're in my seat.'

He was avoiding my eye so I grabbed him by the shoulder.

'Leave it, Jim. You sit in my seat. There's an empty one next to Colin,' Malcolm offered.

Begrudgingly, I sat down and buckled up. Once everyone was settled and the captain started his address, the two soldiers left the plane.

'Were they something to do with you, then?' I asked Khalid.

He finally gave me some eye contact and nodded. I let the subject drop until we were safely airborne.

'Ok, out with it, Khalid. Why did guards bring you onto the plane?'

He mumbled something about disagreements at his site. We hadn't bumped into each other at the hotel or the airport which seemed a bit odd. Maybe he was isolated from us.

'So you were on the human shield then?'

'Yes,' he said.

'Khalid, you're beginning to annoy me and if you don't want me to throw you out of my seat, you'd better explain about the soldiers.'

He said that there was some unpleasantness and since then he had been under guard.

'Did the guards give you a lot of trouble?'

'It wasn't the guards. They were ok. It was the other British expats I had a problem with,' he answered.

There was more to this story than met the eye but I decided to let the matter drop for the time being.

The atmosphere on the plane resembled a jolly boys' outing. Many had somehow managed to acquire alcohol and the plane was also well stocked. Drinks were paid for in US dollars, British pounds or German deutschemarks. I found it hilarious that Iraq Airways refused to accept their own currency. A strong community spirit prevailed and men who had booze were generously sharing with those who did not. The plane climbed and a bottle, two-thirds full of Stolichnaya vodka, rolled to a stop against my feet. When we stabilised, I stood up and shouted forward, 'Anyone missing a bottle of vodka?'

No one claimed it so we passed the bottle around. There were as many men milling around the aisles catching up with friends as there were seated, and it felt like a party was in the offing. A man squeezed his way up the aisle from the rear of the plane and asked, 'Are you a friend of his?' he pointed at Khalid.

'Not really. He was a work colleague.'

'We're going to tear him apart!' he threatened.

'Oh right. I guess you are the reason for the soldiers.'

'Turns out he was reporting to the guards everything we said. We planned an escape and he told them all about it. He's fucking history!' the man exclaimed.

'Yes, well, quite possibly, but nothing is going to happen until we land, is it?'

The man gave me a stern look as if I was challenging him.

'Look, pal, you can't cause any sort of a ruckus while the plane is in the air and, to be honest, I'll have to defend him.'

'Fair enough. When we are back in the UK it is, then,' he said and disappeared back down the aisle.

I resumed my seat to have a little chat with Khalid.

Our own escape plan might have been pitiful but at least it had helped us to stay positive. The idea that he had informed on his fellow hostages outraged and disgusted me.

'I've just been told you informed the guards about your group's escape plan.'

175

'Yes, I did. Their plan was completely ridiculous with zero chance of success,' he blurted out.

'Fine. I accept the plan was likely to fail but why tell the guards?' I asked.

'Because it was a dangerous plan that might have got us killed,' was his reply.

Khalid was an Oxbridge scholar who possessed a brilliant mind. However, he was a loner who lacked any sort of empathy for his fellow human beings.

'You're a clever guy, Khalid. Couldn't you have reasoned with them? What did they say when you told them you were going to the guards?'

'I didn't speak to them and I didn't tell them I was reporting it.'

Purely because I was aware of his character, I was not as shocked as I should have been. In his mind he hadn't informed the guards because he was a coward, scared, or wanted some sort of reward. He had ratted out his fellow hostages because their plan didn't make any sense to him. Knowing his personality, maybe I was the only man on the plane who could feel any sympathy for his stance, but I was not feeling it! Any understanding was tempered by revulsion at what he had done.

'You should have spoken to them – tried to sort things out. Anyway, we are where we are. You can relax on the plane but when we get home, you need to watch your back. I talked with one of your group and they're really pissed off with you.'

This was our flight to freedom and I wanted to enjoy it. Determined that Colin, Malcolm and I should enjoy a tot of vodka together as a celebration, the remains of the Stolichnaya and I made our way to their seats.

'Good evening, gentlemen. I believe a celebratory slug of vodka might be the order of the day.'

I drained the bottle into three good size measures. My proposed 'Bottom's up!' was met with 'Cheers!'

'What was going on with your friend?' Malcolm asked.

'He's just a work colleague.'

After relating his story and trying to explain his peculiarities, they were visibly shocked. There was no arguing – he had behaved in a despicable manner.

One of the guys I had met in the hotel bar distracted me with a can of beer and we were schmoozing in the aisles when a steward asked us to take our seats. He was met with a cat-call of expletives, and bristled, 'We are coming to Heathrow but will not land if everybody is not sat down,' he admonished us.

We returned to our seats with growing excitement, both relieved and elated, knowing that the long wait was over.

'Who is meeting you when we land?' I asked Khalid.

'No one. I will make my way to my brother's. He is letting me stay for a couple of days.'

Some years later Khalid called and asked me to lunch. The food arrived and I was still waiting for his pitch. I wrongly assumed the contact was of a business nature. No! He called because he considered me one of his few friends. It is sad to think that he believed us to be friends entirely because I was not openly hostile to him. Unfortunately, the man's brilliant mind was not completely balanced.

(Khalid ventured onto a moor one day with a container full of aspirin and a bottle of whisky. According to the newspaper obituary, he died of exposure. I was sad at the passing of this lonely man, and occasionally reflect on the waste. He was one among several suicides committed by the returning men.)

Ping! Ping! The no-smoking and buckle-up signs lit up. The plane was ready to land.

19
Freedom and Home

Freedom and Home

Brave, strong or scared
Who cares?
Each searching within
We cry hope!

Some with absolute faith
Like a bright light
Some dimming
Gone jellied, waiting.

Each strong man
Returning home
Truth always right
Careful of our demons.

Freedom and home
Children and joy of life

Daddy, daddy we love you
While the old ones snooze
The children understand.

The next few hours were an emotional rollercoaster. The airport authorities got it right. Considering the occasion, and potential for disaster, things moved very smoothly. Someone, somewhere, used their brain and our arrival was organised with proficiency and sensitivity. The usual scrutiny at passport control was eased and we passed into a hall where only family members were permitted. This allowed us to embrace them shielded from the press.

Mandy held a sleepy Charlotte in her arms and, together with my father, they stood waiting to meet me. As I approached them, I saw the shock on their faces, apart from my daughter who didn't recognise me at all. My hair and beard were long and, due to the significant weight loss, my clothes swamped me. We were overwhelmed with emotion and with the realisation that I was finally safely home. My legs turned to jelly as an invisible millstone fell from my shoulders. Managing to stay upright, I held them and told them that I loved them as the tension of the last four months drained away.

The following week or so was spent at my in-laws house and I struggled to settle. People who knew that I had returned from Iraq gazed at me with expressions usually reserved for freak shows. Life was not moving forward for me as I imagined it might. Like a movie where the dubbing is off or the film itself is misaligned, I struggled to follow the plot. Family and friends made allowances and pussy-footed around me.

There was no eureka moment during the long hours of

Home at last with Charlotte.

incarceration but a slow realisation that I was truly alive. My thinking may have been irrational but I believed that most people were only half alive. They were going through the motions, so to speak, and that, prior to the invasion, I was one of them. Not now, of course – now I felt different.

There was a more feral quality to me and I was restless. Missing the adrenalin rush and atmosphere of Baghdad, I considered approaching the BBC or the like and going back. It would be at their expense naturally! My Arabic was sketchy but I could make myself understood. First-hand experience and knowledge might be of interest to them if they wanted to put a team into Kuwait. I knew the city, the streets, and had solid contacts amongst the locals. In my mind, I would be well worth employing on a three-month contract. The idea was always going to be a non-starter because I faced responsibilities at home and had already put Mandy through enough heartache.

With hindsight it is clear a good many of the hostages returned with PTSD (post-traumatic stress disorder) although back in 1991, I'm not sure we knew what that meant. Over time I realised that the best therapy was a return to gainful employment. I joined the support group HOME (Hostages of the Middle East) primarily to gain information while preparing a claim for compensation against Iraq but found myself taking help in many other ways. I attended one of their functions and met plenty of ex human shields. All those who returned to work seemed to have recovered from their ordeal, at least on the surface. Those that had not were still basket-cases climbing the walls, and I include myself in that category. I believed that once back to a daily routine and given another focus, we should regain a sense of proportion.

The Americans were offered one to one counselling and help returning to work was provided where necessary. We received nothing from our government. Oh, I tell a lie – within a week of my return, I received a poll tax bill. A few of the returning Brits committed suicide and I wonder how those statistics compared with the US figures. The government shamelessly used us for their media propaganda during the crisis but we had now passed our sell-by date.

A return to our flat brought no respite to my feeling of disconnection. I believed that I was fine but my behaviour suggested otherwise. My brother and a few friends arranged to meet up in London for drinks. There was no way that I felt up to taking a bus and tube so I ordered a taxi from the office at the end of my road.

The driver's radio was tuned to a news channel and we listened as the military build-up readied itself for war. Fighting was inevitable and I thanked my lucky stars that I was no longer on the human shield. One pundit was talking nonsense and I started swearing at the radio in Arabic. When he was a boy, the cabby had fled Iran during the time of the revolution, and the family settled in the UK.

'So you speak some Arabic?' he commented.

'I just spent three years in Kuwait and only learned a few words. I've learned a lot more over the last three months in Iraq.'

We arrived at a side street near Charing Cross station and I told the driver that I was not going to pay the fare.

'You have to pay. Everybody has to pay.'

'No, I don't. You people have taken enough from me.'

I believed what I was saying at the time but obviously it made no sense. For a start the driver came from Iran, not Iraq – as if that was the only flaw in my reasoning! He asked me to wait while he located a policeman. As soon as he was out of sight, I made my way onto the Strand. At the time, it never crossed my mind that the cab driver knew where I lived and might return with a few colleagues demanding payment. I am not proud of the way I behaved, but it was what it was. The taxi driver must have decided to let the matter drop.

Quite often, since my return, I found myself with a raging thirst. Feeling completely dehydrated, I took a large bottle of water from the fridge of a newsagent's. A worker from the shop caught up with me close to where my brother worked.

'Excuse me. You have forgotten to pay.'

'No, I haven't. I'm not paying for water.'

Steve came bounding over. Fortunately he was on his way to

meet me. 'I'm sorry. My brother has just returned from Iraq. He was a hostage there. How much do I owe you?'

The lady gave me the look that I was beginning to get used to and made all the right cooing noises.

Mandy was kind and caring while I dwelt in a twilight zone. She put up with all my nonsense without complaint and then she had to put up with some more – Bushby was coming to stay! Once he had claimed the sofa of our one bedroom flat, he settled into a routine. Suited and booted, he left in the morning and roamed the city hand delivering CVs and visiting head-hunting agencies. Around five o'clock he usually visited the bars and collected as many business cards as he could. You had to give the boy credit – he had the right aptitude and application. Less than a week into his visit he called me, 'Hi, chief. You've got to get yourself up here. I'm in a pub near Fleet Street and these press people are buying the drinks.'

'I bet they are! Have you told them your story?'

I already knew the answer before he came back with, 'Of course and I told them all about you as well. Come on! Free beer, mate!'

My Canadian friend could be quite brilliant when sober but, once drinking, things could quickly deteriorate.

When I arrived, Bushby was the centre of attention at the bar. He introduced his drinking companions who were employees working for newspapers and magazines.

'Is this bloke for real? I mean, he's had a few,' one of them asked me.

'I don't know. What has he told you?'

'He reckons he's just returned from Baghdad.'

The man looked at me and decided it was true.

'You must be his mate who was on the human shield.'

They plied us with both drink and questions and I was tiring of it. It felt like a grilling but Bushby was happy enough to sit at the bar. He was now deep in conversation with a prostitute. They got on like a house on fire and she happily admitted to him that she got paid by the gutter press on occasions to seduce a drunk. He thought it hilarious and said best he get drunk then which made the young lady giggle. I retreated to a comfortable seat and was chatting away to a couple of people when I got a tap on my shoulder, 'Your mate is getting a pasting at the bar.'

I arrived at the bar and was relieved to see my friend was still upright and swinging punches, but there were four guys jabbing away at him. I clouted one standing between the two of us just as the police burst in. The landlord pointed at Bushby and the officers started moving towards him. He was still in the affray and swung around violently in reaction to a punch. Unfortunately, he caught a policewoman by accident and she went flying. The officers threw themselves at the drunken brawler and placed him in handcuffs. I believed there was still a chance of returning home at a decent hour when the landlord shouted to a copper, 'He's with him. He's part of it.'

Marvellous I thought – not back two minutes and I'm captured again!

At Snow Hill station, the city police charged Bushby with a breach of the peace and, more seriously, of assaulting a police officer. They threw him in a cell for the night. Having consumed far less alcohol than my friend, I was able to plead my case and was released with a warning.

The following day, Bushby explained that the journalist concerned with the working girl was getting steamed up over the good time she was having and, when they both started to take the piss out of him, he snapped and head-butted the girl. My mate floored him with a punch and it all kicked off. The woman police officer very kindly made an appearance and explained that the attack on her was not deliberate, which was taken on board by the magistrates. He pled guilty, was bound over to keep the peace and given a fine. His details were: no fixed abode and no current employment. When offered terms, and asked how he wished to pay, 'Do you take gold card, chief?' was deemed an inappropriate response and his fine was increased.

Bushby left us after his court appearance. Taking a leaf out of his book I signed on with the head-hunters and started applying for work. My previous employer settled in full through their rep office in the City but the funds would not last long without a monthly pay-packet coming in. The mortgage alone was costly with interest rates at thirteen percent.

A short while later I decided to visit my father in the New Forest for a few days. He lived in New Milton with a station on the line between Waterloo and Bournemouth. As I walked to the bus stop, two middle-aged ladies were on the pavement approaching. They were about thirty yards away when I noticed them staring. They muttered to each other and crossed the road. I still appeared gaunt and the unkempt beard didn't help.

That evening dad and I talked at length and I let him know of my frustration and struggle to adjust to life back in the UK. He was twelve and living in London when the Second World War broke out, and could sympathise. The following day Mac and a few friends collected me.

'Dad, I'll stay the night in Bournemouth and give you a ring tomorrow.'

We crawled a few pubs and ended up at the Cricketers. Back at Mac's I was grabbed and they made a great show of tying me to a chair. My friend caught my eye. 'You ok, Jim? It's time for the beard to go, mate. You look like a serial killer.'

'It isn't going to be a five-minute job! Look at the length of it,' said Nigel who had once been an apprentice barber.

Alcohol may have played a part but the time was right – the beard had to go.

'Yeah, it's all good. Get rid of the fucker! Mac, make sure you keep it, though. Put it in an envelope or something.'

My friend was happy enough to get my consent and didn't question my request. The following day, I reduced him to hysterics. We sellotaped Abdul's address to a manila envelope filled with my beard and, after a visit to the post office, sent it on its way.

20

Full Circle

The government was not quite finished with me. The phone rang and a well-spoken chap introduced himself as military.

'I'm sure we won't have to bother you. It's more a matter of routine. Could I ask you some questions?'

Our conversation took longer than both of us had imagined as I relayed information I had acquired from Colin on our bus journey to Baghdad. He seemed particularly interested in the moving scrapyard resembling a tank formation.

'Ok, well as I said, we probably won't contact you again.'

They called back. 'Mr Payne, the information you gave us corresponds with our intelligence. Could we meet? We would be happy to come to your home.'

They arrived mob handed. I recalled two from Military Intelligence and two military policemen. One of the policemen left Baghdad with all the women when Saddam asked his son what he wanted for his birthday and received the reply, 'I want my daddy to come home with us.'

He told me he was embarrassed and a little guilty to be flying off with the women and children but also very relieved.

Recognising the Mutla Ridge on a map, I was able to point out the various military positions we had discussed. They showed particular interest in the ack-ack gun placements and asked what type they were. Not having a clue, they produced a large portfolio case similar to those used by artists to carry sketches. They started flipping photographs until I picked one that I thought looked the closest.

I received one more phone call from a man who was collecting evidence for potential war crimes trials.

'I've nothing to say, mate. I'm really not interested in getting involved with anything like that.'

'Fair enough, Mr Payne. We won't contact you again.'

1991 was passing by and I was finding life a lot easier. A feeling of being in limbo was still ever present but that was largely due to a lack of employment. I ignored the one year anniversary of the invasion but, six days later, on 8 August 1991, I met up with Steve and we went to the Oval for the first day of the test match against the West Indies – a match England won by five wickets. An outing to the cricket with my big brother and I thought that the wonderful day couldn't be topped when I discovered it could. The tannoy made an announcement: 'John McCarthy has been released. His plane touched down ... '

I missed the rest of the announcement as a myriad of thoughts jostled around in my head. I almost cried with joy. The strength of my emotion was completely irrational and unexpected but you can't help how you feel. I was caught up in the huge cheer and rose from my seat clapping along with all the other spectators. Turning my head, I caught Steve staring at me. Giving him a smile and a wink, I said, 'The Guvnor!'

We both laughed. Steve knew of my immense respect for all

the Beirut hostages and for John McCarthy in particular.

The human shield was a horrible experience but at least the men and women involved knew there was a timetable and the clock was ticking. The hostages in Beirut underwent such savage treatment that using the same word 'hostage' to compare their endless ordeal with our predicament, was ridiculous. If the press wanted to call us hostages, then they had to find a whole new vocabulary for those brave men who survived Beirut.

The summer was enjoyable but we didn't go away on holiday as I was worried about unemployment. I needed to go back to work instead of spending all my savings from the past three years. Through job ads in the papers and head-hunters, I went on one fruitless interview after another. During one I came close to punching the interviewer and only stopped myself with great restraint. The gap in my CV since August 1990 was explained in a paragraph. There were a great deal of interviews, particularly in January and February, always the same:

'Tell us your story.'

'What about the job? Can we discuss targets and limits?'

'Don't worry about that just now. Did you meet Saddam?'

My funds were low as we moved through autumn and I considered a change in career maybe even signing-on and seeing about help with retraining when I was contacted by a head-hunter.

'Would you be able to attend an interview this week?'

'Yes, sure, but I think we should charge them.'

'What!' he exclaimed.

'I keep going to these interviews and they have no interest in employing me. It's a wind-up. They just want to hear my story and I think they should pay me for my expenses.'

He sighed, 'This one's different, Jim, I promise you.'

He went on to describe Colin who had worldwide experience in senior banking management. He was the CEO of a bank in Paris during the time of my incarceration. His intelligence, wit and drive were matched with a true empathy for people, something not often seen in the banking profession. He had arranged a family holiday for the previous summer when Saddam changed Colin's plans. His family still enjoyed their break but he returned to London and manned a phone for the Gulf Link Support Group. He had since parted ways with the French and taken employment as the Treasurer of a bank in Riyadh, Saudi Arabia. He was looking for someone to run foreign exchange. Colin heard about me and wanted to help if he could. I found him very likeable and we talked at length about people we both knew and, of course, my experience of the previous year. He moved the interview to a more professional footing and, after twenty minutes, said, 'Oh dear, you really aren't doing very well. I think the best thing we can do is get you back to work.'

We thrashed out the details of the contract and he promised to have it in the post by the following day.

With mild trepidation I prepared for life in the desert once again. Excitement overcame my worries and I looked forward to being back in the Middle East.